The Limitations of Language

Terence Moore and Chris Carling

First published 1988

Published by
THE MACMILLAN PRESS LTD
Houndmills, Basingstoke, Hampshire RG21 2XS
and London
Companies and representatives
throughout the world

Printed in Hong Kong

British Library Cataloguing in Publication Data
Moore, Terence
The limitations of language.
1. Language and languages
I. Title   II. Carling, Christine
400   P121
ISBN 0–333–37152–6 (hardcover)
ISBN 0–333–37153–4 (paperback)

THE LIMITATIONS OF LANGUAGE

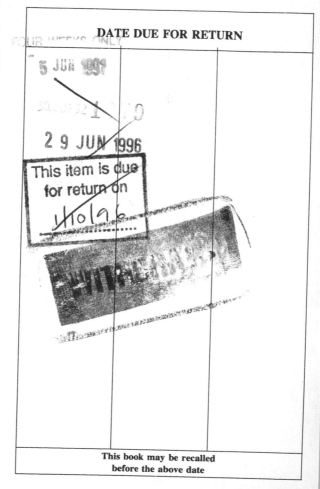

Also by Terence Moore and Chris Carling

*UNDERSTANDING LANGUAGE: Towards a Post-Chomskyan Linguistics

*Also published by Macmillan

Contents

Preface   vii

PART I   LIMITS OF LANGUAGE

1   Changing Perspectives   3

2   Maps and Languages   16

3   Languages and Maps   19

4   The Public and the Private: a difficult balancing act   25

5   Secret Reference: a grand illusion?   31

6   Words and Things: a second secret reference   37

7   Convergence   45

8   Convergence and Clarity   50

9   Taking Time to Understand   59

10   Private Uncertainty, Public Confusion   66

11   Language on Automatic Pilot   71

12   Language Solidarity   77

PART II   LANGUAGE, SENSE AND EMOTION

13   Seeing Faces   85

14   When a Face Really Matters   96

15   **Educating the Senses**   101

16   **Talking about Tasting: the language of wine**   110

17   **Wine and Words: an empirical approach**   121

18   **Feeling We Understand**   126

19   **Language and Emotion**   133

PART III   THE LANGUAGE OF REFLECTION

20   **Taking Part and Standing Back**   145

21   **Telling Stories: a special case of observer language**   158

22   **Telling Stories and Telling the Truth**   164

Coda   173
References   174
Index   179

Preface

Most of us at one time or another have felt let down by language, have felt misunderstood or been unable to express at all adequately what is in our minds. One reason may have been that we expected too much of language, too readily took it for granted we would understand and be understood, too easily forgot that, as a means of communication, language is only a fragile bridge prone to collapse when subject to strain.

In writing this book we wanted to look at language from a fresh perspective, beginning by acknowledging that, imprisoned as we ultimately are within ourselves, communicating with one another by means of words is an inherently difficult task with no guarantee of success.

One of the ways we can make the task easier is by becoming much more conscious of the strengths and, more particularly, the limitations of language: what we cannot easily say, what we should not even expect to be able to say. Recognising the limitations of language is not the same as overcoming them – they can never be wholly overcome, only diminished. Nevertheless, the more we are aware that language is in the end no more than a rough and ready, imperfect instrument, the greater the likelihood of our understanding and being understood.

There are obvious hazards, absurdities even, in attempting to write a book about the limitations of language in language. At the best of times using language to talk about language is rather like engaging in a civil war and being on both sides at the same time. In using language to talk about the limitations of language, however, both sides are likely to be fighting a losing battle. Perhaps it would have been wiser to remain silent.

In writing the book we have been considerably helped by people from a range of professions – solicitors, social workers, marriage guidance counsellors, police – who have talked freely with us and answered patiently our seemingly obvious questions. We gratefully acknowledge their help. We should also like to thank Oxford University Press for permission to reproduce sections of the Clarendon Press (1975) edition of John Locke's *An Essay concerning Human Understanding*, edited by Peter H. Nidditch.

Cambridge TERENCE MOORE *and* CHRIS CARLING

Part I
Limits of Language

'Speech is a joint game between the talker and the listener
against the forces of confusion. Unless both make the
effort . . . communication is quite hopeless.'

Norbert Weiner, *The Human Use of Human Beings*

1
Changing Perspectives

Wittgenstein tells a story of a man's attempt to escape from a room. First he tries the window, locked and barred, then the chimney, then a panel leading to a secret passageway, but all to no avail. He sits down in despair, head in hands. Then he notices that the door has been unlocked all the time.

Conceptual confusion is like that. We follow trails that turn out to be false; come to dead ends or run, sometimes headlong, into brick walls. Yet all the time, if we could only shift our perspective, there is an alternative, a way out, another way of looking at the problem.

Before embarking on this book, we had come to feel something of the frustration of Wittgenstein's prisoner. We wanted to understand how it is that on some occasions language works perfectly well and on other occasions perfectly badly. We looked in what seemed like all the obvious places. We read the work of fellow-linguists, of philosophers of language, of cognitive psychologists, of researchers in artificial intelligence who claimed to throw light on the workings of language.

Naturally we found much that was stimulating, and some that was not. What we also found was an implicit acknowledgement that none of us really understands our capacity to communicate through language. The knowledgeable know that there are no satisfying answers to the apparently simple questions that continue to nag at us: how communication works, why it works, whether on some occasions we should expect it to work at all.

We all know, of course, that in talking with certain people at certain times, we appear to be getting through, making contact. But we rarely stop and ask ourselves: why? What was so special or ordinary about these people, this relationship, this occasion?

Instead of stopping to ask, we ordinarily take success for granted, see it as normal, run of the mill. Worse, we expect other conversations with other people on other days to run as smoothly.

3

Feel let down, disappointed, even a sense of failure when they do not.

What we do not see is that much of the time we expect too much of language. We fail to see how it is double-edged. We fail to see that words can both enlighten and confuse. Inspire and mislead. We fail to see that words can both help us impose some order on our experience of living while at the same time deceive us into believing this order is greater than it really is.

Because nearly all of us expect too much of language, we are not sufficiently alert to its limitations. Not aware of the inexpressible, what we cannot say, what we should not expect to be able to say. Not aware of the vagueness and uncertainty that clouds much of our understanding. Not aware that language only enables us to communicate with one another when the conditions are right. Not aware of the emptiness of language when they are not.

Why, we wondered are we so resolutely unaware? Why do we have such high expectations of language? Where do they come from? How justified are they?

Faced with no obvious answers to these persistent questions, we gradually came to realise that, like Wittgenstein's prisoner, we too had been looking in the wrong places. In practice the door could be opened, though where it would lead was another question. The key, curiously enough, we found in the work of John Locke – in Book III of *An Essay concerning Human Understanding*.

Before that key could be effectively used, however, we had, like Wittgenstein's prisoner, to realise the possibility of changing our perspective. For us the shift began on a longish walk, a walk on which the seeds of this book were sown. It began as quite an ordinary walk but turned out in the end to be extraordinary.

We are keen fell walkers, reasonably experienced now. But there was a time when we would stride off into the Peaks or the Lakeland Fells with a map, but without a compass, only to end up entirely lost charging across bogs, running to avoid sinking in too far. Fortunately we wore tough, no-nonsense army surplus boots that shrugged off water and seemed to thrive on mud.

Many of those early expeditions have sunk into oblivion, but one, the saga of South Head, we have not wanted to forget. We were in the Pennines at the Peak District end. We had left our car in the village of Hayfield and set out with rucksacks stocked with food and thermoses on a circular walk we had planned from an Ordnance Survey map.

We were to go south first but only for a very short way as far as Coldwell Clough, then east to Edale Cross by Jacob's Ladder; there we would turn north on to the Pennine Way, north west at Kinder Downfall, and eventually complete the circle by coming back down William Clough, passing above Kinder reservoir before regaining the village.

It was August and a fine day. A weekday in a holiday month. We set off along a well-defined track which our map told us should remain well-defined for about two-and-a-half miles, probably more – that is until we were fairly near Edale Cross where we were to join the Pennine Way. At this early stage in our walking career we had never been on the Pennine Way, but we had heard how it was heavily used. We had visions of suddenly coming upon streams of hikers – the Piccadilly of the Peaks.

Not that as yet we had seen anyone at all. We marched along cheerfully, fresh and optimistic as we always were at the start. After about half an hour we passed through a farm at a point where the track took a turn. We consulted the map. There was a farm on the map alright, marked South Head Farm, but it was somewhat to the south of our track. So this couldn't be South Head Farm. We looked again more closely. There, where the track marked on the map, our track, turned east, was a tiny grey square – didn't that generally mean 'building'? That grey square on the map must be this farm. Funny though, we thought we had gone further than that. According to the map we still had more than a mile-and-a-half to go to Edale Cross with the prospect of Jacob's Ladder and the streams of hikers. But at least it was a mile-and-a-half along a track which looked as though it should be well-defined.

And so we marched on. Only before very long the well-defined track became an ill-defined track which then all but petered out. We weren't unduly perturbed. Tracks had petered out on us before. We could see from the contour lines on the map that we should be climbing, and ahead there was certainly a steepish-looking slope with something which may very well have been a track wending its way up the side.

So we soldiered on steeply, through longish grass. The fine day had become a hot day, and there were lots of flies about which can be a hazard when you're panting and have to open your mouth to gulp in extra air. The 'track' had quickly proved itself to be a sheep run.

But at least we were near the top, or so it seemed. Only it was one of those illusions you get used to when you walk a lot in the hills. What looks like *the* top turns out to be merely *a* top, a stage on the way to another 'top' and another. . . Funny, the contour lines on the map hadn't looked all that close together. We hadn't expected the climb towards Edale Cross to be so steep.

Finally, after much sweating and many flies, we emerged to our relief and delight at a junction, our non-existent path joining a broad track. The Pennine Way this, surely. No sign of the streams of hikers though. And if this were Edale Cross, shouldn't there be a cross?

There wasn't. But what there was, just up ahead, was a small summit that looked eminently climbable and could only be Jacob's Ladder. We decided to have our lunch on top.

Munching our ham rolls we surveyed the countryside stretched out before us with a certain satisfaction. That stiff climb had been tough . . . well, toughish . . . and what with the path petering out . . . this map really was not reliable.

Drinking our coffee we looked at the map again, and again at the countryside stretched out below us. According to the map, if we looked right we should expect to see a path leading off into the hills towards Kinder Scout. To our left we should see another summit, this one called Brown Knoll. We looked right. There was a track alright, the one we had been so relieved to see when we emerged from our climb. But far from stretching away into the hills, it appeared to lead down to a road. The same track going in the opposite direction was visible when we looked to our left. There was, however, no sign of Brown Knoll. Instead, another road.

We peered harder at the map, willing it to make some sort of sense until one of us voiced what we had both begun thinking: 'Maybe this isn't Jacob's Ladder after all.' But if we weren't at Jacob's Ladder, where were we?

According to the map Jacob's Ladder was about two-and-a-half miles, certainly no more than three miles, due east of where we had started. Had we somehow managed to overshoot it, or go round it, or . . . ? We scrutinised the entire eastern section of the map trying to make it fit the terrain we saw around us, the track and the two roads which were undeniably there whatever the map said. But we failed. The only roads within striking distance of where we had started were to the south.

And we certainly hadn't been going south. Or had we? We looked again at the map and at the roads, and it slowly dawned on us that we might have to abandon entirely the view that had sustained us up to now, the view that we were walking in an easterly direction towards Edale Cross and the Pennine Way. The only way the map and the terrain made any sense at all was if we were not due east at all, but instead due south of where we had started so cheerfully and optimistically not so very long before.

Looked at from this new perspective it was obvious we were nowhere near Jacob's Ladder, but on the very lowly summit of South Head. Looked at from this new perspective it was abundantly clear that we had taken a wrong fork almost at the start and that the farm we had passed had indeed been South Head Farm, where, as the map now very clearly indicated, the track did come to an end. So we had looked in vain for a path as we had scrambled up the steep slope in the heat and the flies. There wasn't one, as the map now made perfectly plain.

It was an extraordinary moment of revelation we have never forgotten. Shifting our perspective and suddenly seeing everything fall into place. Order out of confusion. We were entirely taken aback. Not because we had gone wrong. That wasn't at all difficult to believe. But because we had concealed it from ourselves so successfully. We had forged on doggedly, interpreting the world around us the way we required it to be, forcing the terrain to fit our reading of the map, blissfully unaware we were walking an illusion.

Like Wittgenstein's prisoner we had expected the world to conform to our view of it. Only when we gave up our view, or rather exchanged it for another – for there has to be some view – did a door open and a way forward reveal itself.

South Head has stayed with us as a salutary reminder of how easy it is to see the world selectively, to forget that it can look quite different from another perspective, to assume we see it as it *is*; to believe we understand it better than we do.

'South Head' became our way of reminding one another that the world is often not as it seems; that we, each of us, forge our own perspective, our way of looking at things, our way of imposing order on the world around us. And though we often do so on the flimsiest of evidence, relying on hunches and intuitions, we find it nevertheless surprisingly difficult to change our perspective, to see that we may have been misled.

Subsequently South Head took on a much richer significance, helping us to see that we had been tackling problems of language and understanding too from the wrong point of view. If we could go so wrong in interpreting a map, because we failed to see that there could be another perspective, another interpretation, might we not go just as wrong in interpreting what others said or wrote? Failing to remember that they might see the world in a quite different way, that their words – though apparently the same as ours – might have another, quite different interpretation. Might others too be wandering equally astray in understanding us?

Languages, it struck us, are in some respects like maps. If each of us sees the world from our particular perspective, then an individual's language is, in a sense, like a map of their world. Trying to understand another person is like trying to read a map, their map, a map of the world from their perspective. And as we well knew, map-reading is a craft, a skill. Some of us learn to do it better than others.

As maps can mislead and confuse, the more so if used without a compass, so too can language. Particularly if we expect too much of it, forget the different perspectives. Particularly if we exaggerate its strengths, fail to see its inherent limitations.

But if this is a book about the limitations of language, it is not so much about how to overcome them – they can never be wholly overcome – as about how to understand them. It is a book that may in the right hands serve as a compass to the use of language, a help in finding bearings when the going gets tough and we seem to have lost the route to understanding others and making ourselves understood.

*   *   *

It is also a book about the paradoxes inherent in language. For becoming alert to its limitations does not mean losing our wonder at the miracle of language: somebody shapes a few noises with their tongue and lips, or scribbles some marks on paper, and if the conditions are right, other people respond, are moved to action or to tears, to excitement, to anger, to compassion, to indignation, to laughter, moved to see things differently, feel things more sharply by patterned noise, structured marks.

Consider Stoppard on making contact:

Opens in pitch darkness
After several seconds of nothing, a voice from the dark . . .

Guildenstern:	Are you there?
Rosencrantz:	Where?
Guildenstern:	(Bitterly) A flying start . . .
(PAUSE)	
Rosencrantz:	Is that you?
Guildenstern:	Yes.
Rosencrantz:	How do you know?
Guildenstern:	(Explosion) Oh, for God's sake!
Rosencrantz:	We're not finished, then?
Guildenstern:	Well, we're here, aren't we?
Rosencrantz:	Are we? I can't see a thing.
Guildenstern:	You can still *think*, can't you?
Rosencrantz:	I think so.
Guildenstern:	You can still *talk*.
Rosencrantz:	What should I say?
Guildenstern:	Don't bother. You can *feel*, can't you?
Rosencrantz:	Ah! There's life in me yet!
Guildenstern:	What are you feeling?
Rosencrantz:	A leg. Yes, it feels like my leg.

Tom Stoppard, *Rosencrantz and Guildenstern are Dead*

Sappho on loneliness:

> The moon has set, and the Pleiades;
> It is midnight and time passes.
> Time passes and I lie here alone.

Sappho, *The Pleiades*

Epicurus on death:

Accustom yourself to believing that death means nothing to us; for good and evil are in our perception of them, but death is the deprivation of all perception. Thus the right understanding of the fact that death means nothing to us makes us capable of enjoying this mortal life, not in setting before ourselves the prospect of boundless time, but in taking away from us the yearning for immortality. For there is nothing terrible in living for him that has truly grasped that there is nothing in the life beyond. Therefore he is foolish who says that death should be feared, not because it will be painful when it comes, but because it is painful to look forward to; for it is vain to be grieved in anticipation of that which distresses us not when it arrives. Thus, that which is the most awful of evils, death, means nothing to us, since so long as we exist there is no death, and when there is death we no more exist. Death then concerns neither the living nor the dead, since it does not exist for the first and the second are no more.

Epicurus, *Epistula ad Menoecum*

Herbert on rejuvenescence:

Who would have thought my shrivelled heart
Could have recovered greenness? It was gone
Quite under ground: as flowers depart
To see their mother root, when they have blown,
     Where they together
     All the hard weather
Dead to the world, keep house unknown.

And now in age I bud again
After so many deaths I live and write;
I once more smell the dew and rain . . .

George Herbert, *The Flower*

Ausonius on withstanding the effects of time:

Uxor, vivamus ut viximus, et teneamus
nomina quae primo sumpsimus in thalamo;
nec ferat ulla dies, ut commutetur in aevo
quin tibi sim juvenis tuque puella mihi.

Ausonius, *Ad Uxorem*

Hopkins on a kind of anguish:

As a dare-gale skylark scanted in a dull cage
Man's mounting spirit in his bone house, mean house, dwells –
That bird beyond the remembering his free fells;
This in drudgery, day-labouring-out life's age.

Though aloft on turf, or perch, or poor low stage,
Both sing sometimes the sweetest, sweetest spells,
Yet both droop deadly sometimes in their cells
Or wring their barriers in bursts of fear or rage.

Not that the sweet-fowl, song-fowl, needs no rest –
Why, hear him, hear him babble and drop down to his nest,
But his own nest, wild nest, no prison.

Man's spirit will be flesh-bound when found at best,
But unencumbered: meadow down is not distressed
For a rainbow footing it nor he for his bones risen.

Gerard Manley Hopkins, *The Caged Skylark*

Stevens on facing reality:

. . . How cold the vacancy
When the phantoms are gone and the shaken realist
First sees reality. The mortal no
Has its emptiness and tragic expirations.
The tragedy, however, may have begun,
Again, in the imagination's new beginning,
In the yes of the realist spoken because he must
Say yes, spoken because under every no
Lay a passion for yes that had never been broken.

Wallace Stevens, *Esthétique du Mal*

Arnold on love:

Ah, love, let us be true
To one another! For the world which seems
To lie before us, like a land of dreams,

So various, so beautiful, so new,
Hath really neither joy, nor love, nor light,
Nor certitude, nor peace, nor help for pain;

Matthew Arnold, *Dover Beach*

Eliot on language:

. . . Words strain,
Crack and sometimes break, under the burden,
Under the tension, slip, slide, perish
Decay with imprecision, will not stay in place,
Will not stay still. Shrieking voices
Scolding, mocking, or merely chattering,
Always assail them.

T. S. Eliot, *Burnt Norton*

Marlowe on the limits of language:

If all the pens that ever poets held
Had fed the feeling of their masters' thoughts, . . .
Yet should there hover in their restless heads
One thought, one grace, one wonder at the least
Which into words no virtue can digest.

Christopher Marlowe, *Tamburlaine*

Language at full strength. Language that can, if we are in the right receptive mood, help us shape in our different ways our response to the bizarre business of living.

Most language though is not so momentous. That is why the miracle of language is in the end puzzling. How can it be that some bits and pieces of spoken and written language come to mean so much to us, while others flow over us barely causing a ripple in our consciousness? This is a book for those puzzled by such contradictions.

It is a book too for those who have found themselves at a loss for words and wanted to understand why, for those who have ever said out loud or inside: 'I can't explain' or 'I don't know what the words are' or 'I don't know how to say this'. Not only at extraordinary moments as when Anatoly Shcharansky, released from eight years in a Soviet prison camp, reportedly said: 'there are such moments in our lives that are simply impossible to describe and feelings that are impossible to express in any language'. But on absolutely ordinary, everyday, mundane occasions: trying to describe the face of a friend or the colour of a sweater seen in a shop window.

Sometimes when we are at a loss for words it distresses us. We can feel let down by language. Not only when words fail us, but when what we say seems to be misinterpreted, misunderstood. We have all engaged in conversations that have floundered, where nothing seemed to gel, where one kept, apparently, saying the wrong thing, never really getting through.

At the same time we have all played the pretend-to-understand language game, acting as if we are listening, all the time nodding, feigning an interest, making encouraging noises, feeling the flow of familiar-sounding words wash over, going through the motions of understanding with only the vaguest idea of what was being said.

This is only one of the fictions surrounding language, the illusions we maintain as we pick up words and phrases we barely understand and use them without being caught out, get carried away by the sound of words, particularly long, important-sounding words, words that lull us into a false sense of understanding what we ill-comprehend. There are many experiences for which we have the words but no real understanding.

More insidious is the way certain types of language can stand between us and a clear sense of what we are talking about:

> . . . This, the crime control model, has a relatively prominent police profile incorporating assertive patrol activity, high level visibility, extensive use of stop and search powers, the likelihood of abrasive street contacts and, on occasions, a casual attitude towards civil rights . . .
>
> An extract from a Metropolitan Police Chief's Annual Report

A reader has to struggle against phrases such as 'assertive patrol activity' and 'abrasive street contacts', struggle to keep in mind that the words refer to real policemen making their presence felt none too gently with real citizens in real city streets. 'Although apparently substantial impact may seem to be gained by such an approach', the Report goes on to acknowledge, 'the long-term possibilities of alienation of the community at large are high, so negating the immediate gains' (1983: 7).

Different kinds of limitations these, which can have serious consequences. What is it about language that makes it possible for words to be so readily loosened from what it is they are being used to talk about?

Understanding how it is that words wash over us sometimes, at others mislead us or let us down, and at others again send our spirits soaring to rapturous heights will not remove the limitations inherent in language or enhance its strengths. But it can help us appreciate more sharply why difficulties arise, why conversing with certain people or discussing certain subjects can pose predictable problems. It can even help us circumvent some of the worst difficulties – sometimes.

To tackle these questions we need a fresh perspective on language. First, we need to be convinced, if we are not already, that attempting to communicate with another person using language is a difficult enterprise. We have to stop taking success for granted. We have to remind ourselves that we are, each of us, ultimately trapped within our own heads, viewing the world from our own perspective, not even letting on most of the time what we understand, or even whether we understand at all. We have to keep firmly in mind that the sounds we string together in the patterns required by our particular language can constitute no more than a very fragile and unsteady bridge between ourselves and other people. A bridge that can certainly be strengthened – by familiarity and routine, by affinities, by love – but a bridge that nevertheless can break.

Second, we need to be convinced that uncertainty and imprecision are inherent in language rather than aberrations to be overcome. It could scarcely be otherwise since the same words and phrases are used by so many different individuals to express so many different attitudes and reactions and experiences.

Accepting imprecision and uncertainty as essential attributes of language does not, however, mean that we cannot try to be clear, to disentangle confused thoughts and cut down vagueness. We can do this better though if we are working with the grain of language, understanding its limitations, rather than against it, aiming for an unattainable exactness.

Once we have accepted doubt and uncertainty wholeheartedly, assented to imprecision, admitted inexactness, it becomes easier to look afresh at the problems of language and understanding.

We began with the story of faulty map-reading. Since maps do, up to a point, provide us with a useful analogy, suppose we begin by looking more closely at maps.

2
Maps and Languages

If languages are, in a sense at least, like maps, then understanding something of the strengths and limitations of maps may help us get a purchase on the problem of understanding the strengths and limitations of language.

Borges called his fable about maps 'Of Exactitude in Science':

In that Empire, the craft of Cartography attained such Perfection that the Map of a single province covered the space of an entire City, and the Map of the Empire itself an entire Province. In the course of Time, these Extensive maps were found somehow wanting, and so the College of Cartographers evolved a Map of the Empire that was of the same Scale as the Empire and coincided with it point for point. Less attentive to the Study of Cartography, succeeding generations came to judge a map of such Magnitude cumbersome and, not without Irreverence, abandoned it to the rigours of sun and Rain. In the western Deserts, tattered fragments of the Map are still to be found, sheltering an occasional Beast or beggar; in the whole Nation no other relic is left of the Discipline of Geography.

Borges, 1975: 131

For the cartographers of that Empire maps in and for themselves came to take precedence over the point and purpose of maps. For students of language the moral is clear: be mindful of the folly of studying language for language's sake. Beware of losing sight of what language is for.

What though are maps? What are maps for?

Maps are representations using symbols and conventions, representations of the world, of the stars, of towns, of tracts of country.

There are street plans, road maps, relief maps, weather maps, Ordnance Survey maps, political maps . . .

All maps have this in common: they are always maps *of* something else. Even a fictional map is a map *of* an imaginary terrain. Maps are adjectival to a world. Maps exist because there are terrains to be charted. Without the terrain, the map itself is nothing, though this isn't always as obvious as it seems.

How do we use maps?

Most commonly we use maps as guides for finding our way around unfamiliar streets or across unfamiliar country. We need a map to explore an unknown terrain.

At the same time maps open up new worlds. By looking at a map we can see the possibility of taking a journey we had not thought to take, we can see how we could go a new way. Maps lead to creativity. We can speculate, we can innovate through maps.

Maps also distort. They have to. Otherwise they would be useless.

For maps to be usable, cartographers must reduce – iron out bends in roads, cut out coves from coastlines. Imagine the alternative: a Borges map so accurate that its scale approaches unity — one mile of the road equal to a mile of the map, every detail of the terrain, every blade of grass represented. A fantasy such as Lewis Carroll too imagined:

> 'That's another thing we've learnt from *your* Nation,' said Mein Herr, 'map-making. But we've carried it much further than *you*. What do you consider the *largest* map that would be really useful?'
> 'About six inches to the mile'.
> 'Only *six inches!*' exclaimed Mein Herr. 'We very soon got to six *yards* to the mile. Then we tried a *hundred* yards to the mile. And then came the grandest idea of all! We actually made a map of the country, on the scale of *a mile to the mile!*'
> 'Have you used it much?' I enquired.
> 'It has never been spread out, yet', said Mein Herr. 'The farmers objected: they said it would cover the whole country and shut

out the sunlight! So we now use the country itself, as its own map, and I assure you it does nearly as well'.

L. Carroll, *Sylvia and Bruno Concluded*, Ch. 11

Yet in reducing, sane cartographers know they must distort. Only by reducing – and necessarily distorting – is it possible to map the whole surface of the earth on a single page in the form of someone's – say Mercator's – projection. Yet such is the distortion that New Zealand on such a projection looks not all that much further from Australia than the British Isles from Europe. 'How long is the bridge that joins New Zealand to Australia?' teachers are said to ask unwary pupils. About the distance from London to Moscow would be an approximate answer.

Only by distorting is it possible to represent undulating terrain on a flat page – by using conventions such as contour lines or colour shading to indicate differences in height.

Reducing too requires selection. Map-makers must decide which features of the terrain to mark with symbols and which to ignore – Ordnance Survey maps mark the position of churches, for instance, but not supermarkets, buildings but not individual trees.

Thus since maps reduce and select and necessarily distort, they must be used with great care, lest we misread the symbols and conventions, fail to take into account the distortion and read into them nonsense. Lest we get lost, confused, end up on South Head when we thought we were at Jacob's Ladder.

3
Languages and Maps

Languages, we suggested, are something like maps.

With a map we represent a terrain, selectively, using symbols, signs and conventions. In language too we use signs and conventions to represent a kind of 'terrain'.

In language, the signs are the words and phrases, the conventions are the patterns in which we order and organise the words – the grammar; the 'terrain' is the people and objects and events, real or imagined, the ideas and feelings and speculations we use the words to talk about.

As maps are of little real importance in themselves, as maps are always maps *of* something else, so too language is always *about* something. The reason we string words together in sometimes quite complex combinations is in the end because there are people and objects, feelings and ideas we want to talk about. Like maps, language is adjectival to a world – though not always an existing world, sometimes a possible world, a world of our creating.

Without 'terrain' of some sort, words are like empty husks, though this is not always as obvious as it seems. Words and phrases can sometimes come adrift from any 'terrain', and once detached can appear to take on a life of their own. We can get carried away by the sounds of words, words with the right ring.

Like maps, language – providing it has not come adrift – can help us find our way, discover patterns and regularities in the welter of confused impressions that constitute our experience of living. We can work out problems, understand complex ideas better by unpacking them in words.

Like maps, language can open up new worlds, we can speculate, we can imagine, we can innovate through language.

But like maps, language also distorts. It has to.

In using language we necessarily reduce and group and select. We encompass millions of people we know next to nothing about in simple phrases such as 'the unemployed' or 'the Third World' or

19

'pensioners', our ideas decidedly hazy as to who individually these 'unemployed' are, or where precisely 'the Third World' is, or what these 'pensioners' actually have in common. We reduce countless different acts by countless different individuals with different aims and motives to simple -isms and -ions: 'vandalism', 'hooliganism', 'dedication', 'devotion'.

This is part of the way language allows us to generalise, to pick out similarities in the situations of different individuals, to gather them under the umbrella of 'student unrest' or 'the disadvantaged', 'the exploited', 'the bosses', 'bureaucracy'. It is one of the strengths of language, one of the ways we are able to transcend our own limited experience of particular bosses, specific cases of bureacuracy; language enables us to draw a more extensive map. Yet dangers lurk here: the danger of believing that just because we have the words, we necessarily understand much about the 'terrain' – what it is we are using the words to talk about.

For language is a double-edged weapon alternately clarifying and confusing. It can help us learn and yet effectively hide our ignorance from us. The newspaper fails to arrive, say, so we ring the newsagent who tells us that there is a strike at the printer's: we learn through language something we did not know before. At the same time language disguises from us how little we really know, allows us to talk with apparent authority about 'strikes' even if we have only the dimmest notions of how industrial relations are carried on, allows us to refer to 'the printer's' with only the most rudimentary idea of what printing actually involves.

The generalising power of language enables us to make impossible maps: to talk of 'mobilising the people' or 'stamping out corruption' or 'eliminating poverty'. It allows us to set fine-sounding goals of 'equal opportunity' or 'a fair deal for the handicapped' or 'rights for ethnic minorities'. We can conquer the world with words without ever changing one iota the sum of human misery, without necessarily knowing what actually would be needed to give the words substance.

Like maps, then, language must be used with great care, lest we forget the reduction, the distortion, lest we confuse the words with the 'terrain', lest we are lured by knowing the words into believing we understand the world itself better than we do. Lest we end up on South Head, believing it to be Jacob's Ladder.

*   *   *

Though languages are like maps in some ways, in one important way they are distinct.

Maps chart the physical world, and as such they are checkable, testable. If there is a footpath on our Ordnance Survey map, but no footpath when we come to walk it, then the map is either out of date – the footpath is now overgrown – or else it is just plain wrong. The great strength of maps is that they are publicly checkable against the terrain they represent.

Language 'maps' are different, only partly checkable against the world around us. Only sometimes do the words we speak or hear relate at all directly to the immediate physical world. Just as often it is the intangible, invisible, immaterial we want to talk about, private feelings, personal attitudes, ideas not yet fully-formed.

Even in the simple cases, when we are firmly fixed in the tangible, the visible, the material world, language 'maps' are rarely straightforward. Take an instance that should be easy: in Clare College, in the university town of Cambridge, England, there is in one of the courts, Memorial Court, a magnificent conifer, tall and imposing with widely-spreading branches. We often point it out to visitors: 'There's a magnificent Douglas fir in the court. You can see it from the study window'.

There is a fragment of a 'language map' that is checkable. Anyone hearing the words can go to the study window and look out at the tree, assess whether the words correspond to what he sees there. This is a case of language being anchored in the external world – though anchors sometimes drift.

Once, though, we had a visitor who looked at the tree, but then demurred: 'That looks to me like a Scots pine'. Yet the physical world had not changed. The tree was the same. What had been brought out into the open was that the language we and our visitor use to talk about trees like this is different. This particular difference was revealed, but purely by chance. Most of the time such differences remain hidden.

As long as we are all standing looking at the tree, it is unlikely to have any consequence that we call it a Douglas fir and he calls it a Scots pine. We may each privately believe the other is wrong and leave it at that. But suppose we had been giving directions by phone: 'You'll know you're in the right court. You'll see a Douglas fir'.

Suppose this same visitor had reached the court and spotted what to him is a Scots pine? Would he go off in search of another

court with another tree, one he would recognise as a Douglas fir?
Or would he assume his Scots pine is our Douglas fir?

The answer is that there is no answer. He will have to judge for
himself. Using language always requires judgement. Judging what
others intend by the words we hear. Judging what others will
understand by the words we use. Like map-reading, language
understanding is a craft. Some of us learn to do it better than
others.

What makes interpreting language more tricky than reading a
map is that there is no key to refer to when we are not sure. No
right answer to the question of what words, phrases, sentences
mean that would do for any instance of their use. Dictionaries can
help but only to a limited extent by giving some clues as to how
individual words have been used in the past. But a dictionary
cannot pronounce definitively on how a particular word or phrase
in a sentence or utterance is being used in the present. Nor can it
prevent us using words in new ways, ways in which they have
never been used before.

Yet if a dictionary would be unlikely to help decide whether our
fir tree is a Douglas fir or a Scots pine – unless it had pictures – an
illustrated book on trees, or a botanist, could surely provide the
'correct' term, the term agreed by conifer specialists for a tree such
as ours.

Probably. 'Correctness' undoubtedly has its place. But it has its
limitations too. Insisting on using the 'correct' term can, in some
circumstances, be as misleading as using the 'wrong' one – as
teachers and pedants frequently discover.

After all, if, to take another example, the Scots and Americans
around you are using 'presently' to indicate 'at present', 'now',
then insisting on using it to mean 'in the not-too-distant future',
'soon' could easily cause confusion. Language is not based on
absolute meanings for words, somewhere laid down. Language is
based on convention, on tacit agreement to use words in similar
ways.

*   *   *

The case of the Douglas fir – or was it a Scots pine? – was meant to
be a simple case of language anchored in the external, physical
world, a case of a 'language map' that was checkable: 'There's a
magnificent Douglas fir in the court . . . '.

But even this was not really a simple case. Using language, it turns out, is rarely simple. It only seems so sometimes when we are talking to particular people, or about familiar subjects. Language involves judgement even when anchored in the external, physical world, even when the words seem testable against the 'terrain'.

How much more room for uncertainty, for differing judgements when it is the intangible, invisible, immaterial we want to talk about. For languages are 'maps' of inner worlds too, of the worlds each of us separately creates when we imagine, believe, suppose, judge, expect, hope, fear . . .

'I believe the spirit of the court dwells in that Douglas fir'.

This is the side of language not at all easily checkable against the 'terrain'; the side of language where judgement is all. Judging what others intend by the words we hear. Judging what others will understand by the words we use.

Because we can use language to talk about what we only suppose, language 'maps' can be maps of what isn't – 'There are gnomes at the bottom of my garden' – of terrae incognitae, of what we would like to be but are not, of what we could be if only things were different.

We can speculate through language: 'Suppose we were to plant another fir'.

We can suffer the loss of that Douglas fir without suffering it: 'Suppose that Douglas fir were cut down'.

Unlike maps which represent a specific terrain, we use language, each of us, individually, to represent two types of 'terrain': an outer, public world, a world of Douglas firs and Scots pines and an inner, intangible, immaterial, invisible private world of feelings and attitudes, ideas and beliefs.

The two are not separate, though in writing about them we have been forced to treat them separately. Rather they are interdependent, our sense of a public world affected immeasurably by the state of our inner world, itself in a constant state of flux.

Notice that we do not say *the* outer, public world, but *an* outer, public world. Each of us must experience even the world around us differently, though fortunately the differences between us are often insignificant. As for the inner, private worlds, there each of us is on our own – which is not to say we do not share many of our hopes and fears and fantasies with others.

So the analogy breaks down. Maps and languages are in the end different because maps are public – the map itself and the terrain it represents are both observable parts of the external world – while languages are both public and private. The words themselves and the conventions whereby we string them to-gether – the grammar – are public, shared, common to those who speak the same language – English, Icelandic, Tagalog, or what-ever – but the 'terrain', what the words and phrases are used to talk about, is only partly public, mostly private.

A group of people speaking English together are only partly speaking the same language. They are using words in structures they will probably all recognise, but the 'terrain' – what it is they are using the words in structures to talk about – may not be the same at all, particularly if they are speculating or expressing their feelings or desires or beliefs.

None of us can ever really know, we can only ever sense or guess, how far we are understood as we intend, how far we understand others as they intend, how far our personal language maps on to a similar 'terrain' to the people we are talking with. Using language involves uncertainty, and it is this which makes linguistic map-reading so tricky. We can so easily go astray. Misinterpret, misunderstand, mislead without realising – forget the possibility of shifting our perspective.

Or we may get it right – understand, explain successfully, make ourselves clear – but without being aware, without being sure we were really getting through.

Trapped in our own heads, we use language to sustain a fragile bridge between ourselves and others. Only it is tempting to forget just how fragile a bridge, how it needs constantly testing and trying and reinforcing, how easily it can break.

4

The Public and the Private: a difficult balancing act

The fragility of the bridge can be traced to a fundamental paradox at the heart of the human condition: each of us lives two lives, one private 'as I', the other public 'as we'. Martin Buber summed it up: 'Experience comes to man "as I" but it is by experience "as we" that he builds the common world in which he lives' (Britton, 1970: 19).

We are, each of us, individuals, separate from one another, different from one another. We have different experience, different memories, different abilities, different dispositions. 'As I' we are alone, separate, knowing what it feels like to be ourselves, incapable of knowing for sure what it feels like to be anyone else.

At the same time we share a great deal with others: knowledge, beliefs, hopes and fears, skills and failings, ordinary human needs for food, shelter, warmth, love, companionship. 'As we' we are part of a common humanity. 'As we', we help build a common world.

The common world we help to build in turn affects our private world, which then affects our contribution to that common world, affecting our private world . . . A constant ebb and flow that makes up the base rhythm of our lives.

The essence of the human condition is to be an odd hybrid, an 'I-we', a public-private thing. To be in part ant-like, bee-like, a member of an organism greater than ourselves; to be in part fox-like, or solitary eagle-like, detached from others of our kind. To be human is to be neither one nor the other but both, simultaneously and indivisibly. Ant and eagle.

This 'I-we', this 'public/private' paradox lies at the heart of our use of language. It was there from the beginning, from our infancy

25

when we somehow began to make connections, set up links
between strings of sounds our parents and the other people
around us were making and our own experience of living.

Their sounds but our experience.

As we came to see patterns in the sounds, as we came to see links
between 'cloud' and the cotton wool in the sky, between 'tired'
and the state we saw our mother in, we stamped a little order on
the 'flux of perceptions, sensations and emotions' that constituted
our experience of living.

The phrase belongs to A. N. Whitehead. 'Actual experience,' he
wrote, 'is for each person a *continuum*, fragmentary, with elements
not clearly differentiated' (Whitehead, 1917: 110).

Language – the strings of sounds made by those around
us – helped us to differentiate some elements, to classify and
categorise, to mark similarities and differences in the flux, to make
some sense out of the fragmented disorder.

Their sounds but our disorder.

Gradually, as we heard their sounds over and over again, as we
used them, combined them in increasingly complex patterns,
gradually their sounds became our sounds.

Our sounds now and our experience.

Gradually, as the chaos began to clear, as patterns and regularities
in our environment emerged, as expectations were established,
where there had been flux, now there was some order. An order
which came in the course of time to seem natural, inherent in the
world, making it difficult to recall that it had been our own private
order that each of us, individually, had imposed as we set up links,
made connections between strings of sounds and our experience
of living.

Making it difficult to recall that it is, ultimately, 'as I' that we
speak and write, 'as I' that we hear and read and try to understand
the language of others. Difficult because it was nevertheless 'as
we' that we learnt to speak and understand, to write and read, that
we acquired our 'language maps'. And it is 'as we', enmeshed

with the lives of others that we constantly reshape and extend and enrich our language along with our experience.

It is this sameness to one another, our living 'as we', that makes communication through language a possibility. It is our difference, our individuality, our living 'as I' that contributes to its breaking down.

* * *

The public/private paradox has another dimension. Experience is not only what happens to us, but equally the way we react and respond to what happens to us.

In learning language, as well as setting up links, making connections, imposing some order on the flux around us, we were at the same time beginning to use the sounds others made to shape a response to what we experienced.

Their sounds in the beginning, but our response.

Some tastes and smells, some sensations, some people and places we liked, some we did not. Sometimes we were at ease, content, at other times less so. We were not neutral to the world. We reacted and felt.

Language – the sounds of those around us – helped us impose some vestige of order on these chaotic feelings and emotions too. As their sounds became our sounds, we were able to use words to discriminate, if often only crudely, the feelings and attitudes and reactions that made up our response to the experience of living.

Our sounds now and our response.

It was not always easy, however, even as we grew older and matured, to translate our response, our feelings and emotions and attitudes into words. Or to be confident if we did succeed, that others, though they shared our language, necessarily understood how we felt.

We feel and respond, we see and smell, we touch and hear and taste, we love and grieve 'as I', though not uniquely. We recognise that others, too, see and taste, crave and fear. Like us, but separately.

At the same time we can affect one another's response – laughter and tears can be infectious. We may be moved by seeing others moved, or we may be uncertain how we feel, adjust our response to correspond with those we respect or admire and strive to emulate.

A question mark hovers over how far we are able to translate into the words we share with others what we feel 'as I'. When we try, how far can others understand the feelings we struggle to express? Even if they do not understand, how far can words help us create some order for ourselves among our tangled emotions? How well are we able to understand others when they try to translate their private experience into words?

A man whose son had just been acquitted on a spying charge after a lengthy trial was asked by a television reporter how he felt: 'I feel like the day I was born'. That was his answer. Though of course he had no way of knowing how he had actually felt on the day he was born. So how *did* he feel? Did he know? Did we, the viewers, then know? Or did we imagine instead how we might feel in his place?

Exploring the relation between language and what we experience through our senses and emotions, we defer to the second part of the book.

It is, however, our sameness to one another, our shared needs, our basic, human hopes and fears, our living 'as we' that makes such communication possible at all. It is our difference, the individuality of our response, the way we feel that others do not, that contributes to its breaking down.

*   *   *

Living involves a constant struggle to get the balance right between the private and the public, the 'I' and the 'we'. A struggle that extends to our use of language where we more often than not get the balance wrong, emphasise one side at the expense of the other.

In the darker moments we have all endured when what we say is twisted or wilfully misunderstood, when we cannot get through at all, when a sense of utter loneliness descends, at such moments it can be tempting to forget the 'we', to cling to the 'I'.

At those times it is only too easy to overemphasise our separateness, to believe that no one else could possibly understand what we are uniquely experiencing.

Such feelings are not without foundation – none of us can *know for certain* what anyone else has in mind by the words they use, or what anyone else understands by what we say.

Yet dwelling too much on the ultimate privateness of meanings can incite radically solipsistic thoughts which, having once trapped us firmly within our own heads, lead to the view that only our own experiences are real.

In two of his last short stories, *The Investigations of a Dog* and *The Burrow*, Kafka grappled with the fate of the extreme solipsist, trapped inside himself, looking outward at a world he is almost wholly isolated from, a world where only he understands his meanings.

Carroll for his part turned solipsism upside down to satirise it. His scornful solipsist strives to keep a fragile integrity by inventing his own, private, meanings for the public words he shares with others:

Humpty Dumpty, sitting on his high narrow wall with his legs crossed like a Turk, arrogantly tried to bemuse poor Alice, a genuine seeker after truth:

'There's glory for you!'

'I don't know what you mean by "glory",' Alice said.

Humpty Dumpty smiled contemptuously. 'Of course you don't – till I tell you. I meant "there's a nice knock-down argument for you!"'

'But "glory" doesn't mean "a nice knock-down argument",' Alice objected.

'When *I* use a word,' Humpty Dumpty said, in rather a scornful tone, 'it means just what I choose it to mean – neither more nor less'.

'The question is,' said Alice, 'whether you *can* make words mean so many different things'.

'The question is,' said Humpty Dumpty, 'which is to be master – that's all'.

L. Carroll, *Through the Looking-Glass*, Ch. 6

Humpty Dumpty was in no doubt who was to be master. He could bend words to his will, make them all serve his purpose, from the proudest, the verbs, to the humblest, the adjectives. He could manage the whole lot of them, he bragged. Yet if he had wanted Alice, or Mrs Dumpty, or the young Dumpties to understand his words, to read his 'map', he would have had to accept Buber's other truth, the 'we' side, the social, public aspect of language.

Otherwise he was condemned to remain astride his wall in splendid, elevated isolation – the ultimate radical solipsist, living only 'as I' by his own, totally private 'language map', comprehensible only to himself. The mocking bully boy, the lonely tyrant of language use, whom Lewis Carroll – himself no radical solipsist – abandoned to his fate.

At the same time exaggerating the 'we' side can mislead just as much as Humpty Dumpty tried to mislead Alice. Concentrating on what binds us to others rather than what keeps us apart, assuming because we use the same words, we necessarily read one another loud and clear, can breed over-confidence in the efficacy of language, blinding us to why it goes wrong.

For Humpty had a point, though Alice was not able to see it.

Whenever we deny the private, whenever we fail to remember that for each of us the words we use and hear relate to 'terrain' we have privately mapped out, forget that we cannot take for granted we are evoking the same 'terrain' just because we are using the same words, then we make it difficult for ourselves to see why language fails to work, why we fail to get through, why we fail to understand, often when we most need to. In place of Humpty's solipsism, simple optimism about the effectiveness of language creates high expectations that are doomed to be dashed.

What is more, the likelihood of forgetting Humpty Dumpty, of altogether denying the 'I' side, the privateness of language maps, is much greater than the likelihood of forgetting the more obvious public, social, 'we' side.

Ordinarily it is easier to fail to remember our aloneness, the 'I' side, than our togetherness – the 'we' side.

So we do often get the balance wrong. Assume communication is easier and more straightforward than it is – take for granted we are understanding and being understood. Forget that language provides only a fragile bridge.

5

Secret Reference: a grand illusion?

Keeping in mind the public and the private cannot guarantee our understanding or being understood – although it undoubtedly helps. The problem lies with the private 'I' side which constitutes the most fundamental limitation on language affecting the degree to which communication is even possible at all.

Caught in a shower we feel the rain falling on us 'as I' – no one else can feel it for us. If others feel it too, then they feel it for themselves. Differently to us, depending on their clothes, their body temperature, their mood.

Every use of language, similarly, has an 'I' side that is inescapable. We speak 'as I' – our voice quality, our accent is ours; no one else speaks exactly as we do. We hear 'as I' – no one else can hear for us. We choose our words 'as I' – and sometimes we are very clear within ourselves what we mean by what we say, and sometimes we are vague, and sometimes we are parrot-like, imitating what others have said. We understand – or not – 'as I', and sometimes we try hard to grasp what others have in mind, while sometimes we barely listen and only vaguely understand.

This is not to say that when others hear us they *may* not understand us more or less as we intend. Or that when we listen to others, we *may* not sometimes grasp quite readily what they have in mind. Communication can seem easy if the conditions are right. But if there are several people listening, they may equally, each of them, understand us differently, depending on *their* mood, *their* wish to understand us, *their* experience, *their* beliefs. And if we ourselves are vague about what we mean – how much more scope then for differences among our listeners.

These observations are only reminders of what we already know. Yet what is remarkable is the way all of us need reminding.

Aware of the inevitable private side to language, we nevertheless fail to see its implications.

One reason we fail may be because the 'I' side, the private side, is very effectively concealed. As English speakers we share common sounds, common words and phrases which are arranged in the conventional patterns, spoken with the conventional rhythms characteristic of our particular language. It is only too easy to assume that the words we speak and hear map by and large on to the same 'terrain' for other people as they do for us. To assume that the words that sound or look the same on the outside are more or less equivalent to the same meanings for each of us on the inside.

One philosopher who did not make this easy assumption was John Locke. Three hundred years ago, in *An Essay concerning Human Understanding*, Locke not only acknowledged a private aspect to language but, unusually, did not shrink from following through its implications for his broader theme: an enquiry into the nature of human (as opposed to divine) understanding.

Locke discovered for himself as he pursued his major theme that:

> there is so close a connexion between *Ideas* and Words . . . that it is impossible to speak clearly and distinctly of our Knowledge . . . without considering, first, the Nature, Use, and Signification of Language; which therefore must be the business of the next Book. (II, XXXIII, 19)

At the outset of his enquiry into the role of language in understanding, Locke outlined a view of meaning which starts by acknowledging the ultimate privateness of meanings.

He begins his account 'Of the Signification of Words' with two pictures. First of a man without a language, locked within his own experience of the world, a radically private man:

> Man, though he have great variety of Thoughts, and such, from which others, as well as himself, might receive Profit and Delight; yet they are all within his own Breast, invisible, and hidden from others, nor can of themselves be made appear. (III, II, 1).

None may know directly another's thoughts.

Next to that picture Locke places another, of man as a social creature, wanting, needing to break out of his isolation, create a 'we' side, a common world with others:

> The Comfort, and Advantage of Society, not being to be had without Communication of Thoughts, it was necessary, that Man should find out some external sensible Signs, whereby those invisible *Ideas*, which his thoughts are made up of, might be made known to others. (III, II, 1)

Communication, Locke saw, brings comfort, comfort in its older, richer sense: a quality that gives strength – *fortis, confortare* – support, encouragement. Communication at the same time is to our advantage, enabling us to learn from others. Trying to get others to understand our thoughts can make them clearer to ourselves.

For man to make known his thoughts to others, render the invisible visible, the silent audible, '. . . nothing was so fit,' Locke went on:

> either for Plenty or Quickness, as those articulate Sounds, which with so much Ease and Variety, he found himself able to make. Thus we may conceive how *Words*, which were by Nature so well adapted to that purpose, come to be made use of by Men as *the Signs of* their *Ideas* (III, II, 1)

Not a serious account of the origins of language. Rather Locke stressing, as Buber does, the significance of the 'we' side, the public side of language. Communication, while difficult, is necessary. Man had to find some way to achieve it.

What makes that task uniquely difficult is that the words we come to use stand, Locke insisted, ultimately for ideas in the minds of individuals; individuals who are, necessarily, separate from one another. As Locke repeated several times in a chapter only four pages long: 'Words in their primary or immediate Signification, stand for nothing, but the *Ideas* in the Mind of him that uses them' (III, II, 2), adding later in the same chapter: 'it is perverting the use of Words, and brings unavoidable Obscurity and Confusion into their Signification, whenever we make them stand for anything, but those *Ideas* we have in our own Minds' (III, II, 5).

Exactly what Locke may have had in mind by 'Idea' is not the important point. He construed it roughly as 'whatever is the Object of the Understanding when a Man thinks . . .' (I, I, 8) – and, rough though his account is, we are still not so very far advanced in understanding better the nature of thought, of meaning and of understanding.

What *is* important is his insistence that in the end no one can apply words '. . . as Marks, immediately to anything else, but the *Ideas* that he himself hath . . .' (III, II, 2). That meanings are ultimately private.

He could just as well have said 'that she herself hath'. Elizabeth Taylor is reported to have said during an interview with film producer Dominick Dunn: 'I think you know how horribly shy I really am' (Dunn, 1986). Dunn does not appear to have probed her use of 'horribly shy'. We cannot know what was in her mind. But we can know that the 'shyness' of a public idol who expects and receives attention, affection, adulation everywhere she goes, must be a special sort of shyness, born of a special sort of life. 'Shy' stands for nothing but the Idea in the mind of her that uses it . . .

It is Locke's emphasis on the privateness of meaning, his insistence that 'words in their primary or immediate signification stand for nothing but the ideas in the mind of him – or her – that uses them' that leads him to the dilemma we all face, the unresolved, and in a careful sense, unresolvable dilemma underlying all language use: its ultimate limitation.

The dilemma is this: we have, as English speakers, broadly the same vocabulary. We use broadly the same stock of words and expressions combined in the conventional patterns of our speech community. Yet when one person says something, produces a string of words with a particular intonation pattern, these words stand as marks for ideas or impressions in his mind. But when another person hears these words spoken, then they stand as marks for ideas or impressions in his, the hearer's mind. Leaving the unresolved question: how, since we cannot look into each other's heads, can we know we are meaning and understanding the same thing?

One answer, the radical solipsist's answer, is simple: irredeemably separate from one another, we cannot know. No one can directly experience another's thoughts. To pretend we can is to deceive ourselves.

In Humpty Dumpty, Carroll took this line of thought to one kind of conclusion:

'I meant by "impenetrability" that we've had enough of that subject, and it would be just as well if you'd mention what you mean to do next, as I suppose you don't mean to stop here all the rest of your life'.
'That's a great deal to make one word mean,' Alice said in a thoughtful tone.'

L. Carroll, *Through the Looking-Glass*, Ch. 6

Locke's answer is both more serious and more subtle than the radical solipsist's. Underlying our use of language, he says, is a tacit communal conspiracy, a pretence. What we all do in practice is simply assume what we cannot know for certain. We, each of us, individually *act as if* the words I apply 'as marks' for ideas in my head, you are applying 'as marks' for the same or similar ideas in yours.

This tacit communal conspiracy, Locke called his first 'secret reference'.

But though Words, as they are used by Men, can properly and immediately signify nothing but the *Ideas,* that are in the Mind of the Speaker; yet they in their Thoughts give them a secret reference to two other things. (III, II, 4)

First, they suppose their Words to be Marks of the ideas *in the Minds also of other Men, with whom they communicate.* (III, II, 4)

We collude with one another, take it for granted, separately and individually, that we are all in the same boat. Rarely coming out into the open.

Locke saw how indispensable this 'acting as if' is: without it communication through language could not proceed: 'For else they should talk in vain, and could not be understood, if the Sounds they applied to one *Idea,* were such, as by the Hearer, were applied to another, which is to speak two Languages' (III, II, 4).

He saw too that it is precisely because we *do* share so much, because of our similarity to one another, because of the public side of the human condition, that this 'secret reference' can be sustained.

And yet – a most important reservation this – necessary and justified though this 'secret reference', this tacit collusion, is to communication, it is at the same time a deep source of misunderstanding and confusion. Not because we make it – it must be made – but *because we so easily forget that we make it*.

Easily forget that we do not *know* but can only *assume* that the words we use are marks of similar ideas in the minds of others. Easily forget that we can therefore never be sure of what our words stand for in others' minds. Uncertainty is intrinsic to communication. Easily forget the inescapable frailty of the foundations of the bridge between ourselves and others.

6

Words and Things: a second secret reference

Frail though the foundations may be, Locke's first secret reference establishes the indispensable condition for the communal conspiracy we are all tacitly engaged in. By supposing that the words I use 'as marks' for ideas in my head, are also 'marks' for the same or similar ideas in your head, the possibility of communicating is born.

The move we make too readily, however, is to assume that just because we have the possibility of communicating using language, we actually do communicate successfully. This is a particularly hasty assumption given the indirectness of the links between words and what we use words to talk about – often known in a kind of shorthand as 'the world'.

We make the links between language and 'the world', Locke suggests, by means of a second secret reference, the second complementing the first:

> But though Words, as they are used by Men, can properly and immediately signify nothing but the *Ideas* that are in the Mind of the Speaker; yet they in their Thoughts give them a secret reference to two other things.
> First, *they suppose their Words to be Marks of the* Ideas *in the Minds also of other Men, with whom they communicate . . .*
> *Secondly* because *Men* would not be thought to talk *barely* of their own Imaginations, but of Things as really they are; therefore they *often suppose their words to stand also for the reality of Things*. (III, II, 4–5)

Supposing our words to stand for 'the reality of things', for things as they really are can seem a perfectly natural assumption. When, for example, we are talking about the world around us, it

37

appears commonsense to suppose the words we use stand for something real, something outside of ourselves, something more substantial than just 'ideas and such in our heads'. Natural assumptions, unfortunately, however, are not necessarily the most useful ones.

In *Gulliver's Travels* Swift satirised a version of the belief that words stand for things that actually exist when he has Gulliver visit the Academy on the flying island of Laputa. While observing the kind of research being carried out there, he is taken to the School of Languages where a project based on a commonsense view of the relation of words to the world is under serious discussion:

We next went to the School of Languages, where three Professors sat in Consultation upon improving that of their own Country . . . An Expedient was . . . offered, that since Words are only Names for *Things*, it would be more convenient for all Men to carry about them, such *Things* as were necessary to express the particular Business they are to discourse on . . .

many of the most Learned and Wise adhere to the new Scheme of expressing themselves by *Things* which hath only this Inconvenience attending it; that if a Man's Business be very great, and of various Kinds, he must be obliged in Proportion to carry a greater Bundle of *Things* upon his Back, unless he can afford one or two strong Servants to attend him. I have often beheld two of those Sages almost sinking under the Weight of their Packs, like Pedlars among us; who when they met in the Streets would lay down their Loads, open their Sacks, and hold Conversation for an Hour together; then put up their Implements, help each other to resume their Burthens, and take their Leave.

> J. Swift, *Gulliver's Travels*, Part III, Ch. V

Swift's fable carries to its logical conclusion the simple, yet natural, belief that words are essentially names for things. If words are names for things, his logic runs, then why not do without the names altogether and use the things instead?

One reason we are tempted to cling to the view that words stand for 'the reality of things', that language is basically a naming process, is that this seems to correspond to much of our ordinary experience. Take the word 'pen'. I have one in my hand, real enough to write with. If I hold up my pen and say 'This is a pen', then to all intents and purposes the word 'pen' does stand for a real thing in my hand. The reality is plain for all to see.

Suppose though I ask you to bring me a pen. You are not going to bring me the one I already have in my hand. You are going to bring me another pen. How are you able to do that unless you have some idea or impression in your mind of what sorts of things pens are? Clearly words are much more than names for things. Much of our ordinary experience is in the end deceptive.

In *Gulliver's Travels* Swift satirised the simple view. Locke, not a satirist but, as he described himself in his *Epistle to the Reader*, 'an Under-Labourer [employed] in clearing Ground a little, and removing some of the Rubbish, that lies in the way to Knowledge' looked for an answer to the question satire leaves unresolved. If words do not name things, what do words do? A question, we might add, not readily resolved since it has exercised philosophers at least since the time of Plato's *Cratylus*.

What is plain, Locke said, is that words 'belong not to the real existence of Things; but are the *Inventions and Creatures of the Understanding*, made by it for its own use' (III, III, 11).

The meanings we give to words: 'the signification they have, is nothing but a relation, that by the mind of Man is added to them' (III, III, 11).

The links between words, these 'Inventions and Creatures of the Understanding', and 'the world', their 'terrain', what we want to use them to talk about, are forged, by each of us, individually, in a phrase Locke turns to over and over again, by means of 'the Workmanship of the Understanding' (III, III, 13).

There is thus no straightforward link between words and even the most concrete of things. For as Locke construes the 'Workmanship of the Understanding', it is 'the Mind that makes the Patterns, for sorting and naming of Things' (III, V, 9).

Language, for each of us, is the product of the mental processes by which we select and organise our personal experience of 'the world' – a world we share with others but experience individually.

From Locke's position the relation of words to 'the world' is complicatedly oblique, the result of which leaves each of us with: '*Words in their primary or immediate Signification* [standing] *for nothing, but the* Ideas *in the Mind of him that uses them* (III, II, 2).

Locke makes two telling observations about these *Ideas*, which together throw light on why the effectiveness of language in the end must be limited: the ideas words stand for are variable for each of us, and the ideas words stand for are vague for each of us.

His favoured example of the unavoidable variability in our individual meanings is the richly-loaded word 'gold':

A Child having taken notice of nothing in the Metal he hears called Gold, but the bright shining colour, he applies the Word Gold only to his own *Idea* of that Colour, and nothing else; and therefore calls the same Colour in a Peacocks Tail Gold. (III, II, 3)

Someone else who: 'hath better observed, adds to shining yellow, great Weight; And then the Sound Gold, when he uses it, stands for a complex *Idea* of a shining Yellow and very weighty Substance' (III, II, 3).

Another adds to these qualities: 'Fusibility: and then the Word Gold to him signifies a Body, bright, yellow, fusible and very heavy. Another adds Malleability' (III, II, 3).

But Locke concludes:

Each of these uses equally the Word Gold, when they have Occasion to express the *Idea*, which they have apply'd it to: But it is evident, that each can apply it only to his own *Idea*; nor can he make it stand, as a Sign of such a complex *Idea*, as he has not. (III, II, 3)

As well as being variable, the 'ideas' each of us individually has are also vague. Vague, Locke says, partly because 'they are collected from the Things, which they are supposed to repre-sent . . .imperfectly . . . or carelessly' (III, II, 2).

Partly too because the 'ideas' many words stand for: 'have no certain connexion in Nature; and so no settled Standard, any-where in Nature existing, to rectify and adjust them by' (III, IX, 5).

In effect, Locke is sounding a warning about the kinds of difficulties to be expected in trying to establish clear-cut and precise links between words and the world of much of our experience.

In the case of certain types of words – words marking ideas collected from the external, physical world – 'how imperfectly soever or carelessly' they may have been collected 'from the things they are supposed to represent', these difficulties, while always leaving some doubt and uncertainty, are not insurmountable.

Our earlier example 'pen' is a case that is apparently straightforward. The 'ideas and such' of pen in my head and in yours are not likely to be entirely identical. If you brought me a quill, I might say that was not what I meant by pen. But a quill is a kind of pen, you may say. *Was* a kind of pen. Sometimes technology moves on, but language does not. Is a quill a pen because once pens were quills? Does an old-fashioned fountain pen still count as a pen? Or a thick felt tip? Is that a 'pen' or a 'marker'?

Yet though there is always room for doubt, though our ideas and impressions of what counts as a pen may well not be identical, in practice such words – words which relate to our perception of the visible, tangible world – give us relatively few problems in use.

If there is doubt, we can always confer: would you call that a pen? Or that? We can bring out into the open our ideas and impressions, examine one or more examples of what might count as pens, establish explicitly a 'common acceptation' for the word among ourselves.

'Pen' is the kind of word marking an idea for which Locke would say we have a 'Settled standard . . . in Nature . . . to rectify and adjust its signification by' (III, IX, 5). Though the word 'pen' stands for an idea or impression, it is an idea or impression that springs directly from our experience of real things, real pens. We can, in Locke's words, 'rectify and adjust' our use of the word 'pen' in relation to the actual objects we see and use.

But only part of language is like this. Only part of language is made up of words and expressions with relatively clear and straightforward links with the external world as we perceive it. The greater difficulties begin when the apparent simplicity of these links with 'the world' lures us into assuming that words in general stand for things that really exist.

This alluring but meretricious assumption has a long history. John Stuart Mill observed:

Mankind in all ages have had a strong propensity to conclude that whenever there is a name, there must be a distinguishable separate entity corresponding to the name; and every complex idea which the mind has formed for itself by operating upon its conceptions of individual things, was considered to have an outward objective reality answering to it.

J. S. Mill, *A System of Logic*

It is doubtless reinforced by our earliest experience of language when words did appear to stand directly for familiar everyday people and objects and activities, real things and events in the world around us. Recent research has confirmed what most of us probably believed: that the great majority of the words mothers use with toddlers relate to common, everyday objects and actions with a physical manifestation.

Yet though part of language may be readily linked to the external world, there remain many, many other words and expressions for which 'the *Ideas* they stand for, have no certain connexions in Nature; and so no settled Standard anywhere in Nature existing, to rectify and adjust them by'. Words which do not correspond to any perceived outward reality. Words for which the ideas they stand for are often very complex and made up of 'assemblages of *Ideas* put together at the pleasure of the Mind, pursuing its own ends of Discourse, and suited to its own Notions' (III, IX, 7).

It is at these words that Locke's warning about the difficulties of linking words to the world as we perceive it is really aimed. Words like 'murder' or 'sacrilege':

What the word Murther, or Sacriledge, signifies, can never be known from Things themselves: There be many of the parts of those complex *Ideas* which are not visible in the Action itself, the intention of the Mind, or the Relation of holy Things which make a part of Murther, or Sacrilege, have no necessary connexion with the outward and visible Action of him that commits either: and the pulling the Trigger of the Gun, with which the Murther is committed, is all the Action, that, perhaps, is visible, has no natural connexion with those other *Ideas*, that make up the complex one, named *Murther*. (III, IX, 7)

Murder requires an act – firing a gun, perhaps, or plunging a knife into a victim's body. Yet 'murder' does not mean 'fire a gun' or 'plunge a knife'. A soldier who shoots and kills is not a murderer. Nor is a policeman, though grieving relatives and outraged friends sometimes say differently.

People are murdered, but 'murder' as an entity does not exist. We have no 'thing' called 'murder' to measure our use of the word against. Instead, we each of us, gather together a complex of ideas which we knot together with the word 'murder'. The knotting together is done by us individually through 'the Workmanship of the Understanding' (III, V, 13). Such complex ideas Locke insists have: 'their union and combination only from the Understanding which unites them under one Name:' (III, IX, 7).

Such names, unlike words like 'pen', lack: '*Standards* in Nature, whereby Men may rectify and adjust their significations; therefore they are very various and doubtful' (III, IX, 7).

Under such conditions:

it cannot be, but that the signification of the Name, that stands for such voluntary Collections, should be often various in the Minds of different Men, who have scarce any standing Rule to regulate themselves, and their Notions by, in such arbitrary *Ideas*. (III, IX, 7)

'Various in the Minds of different Men' – and women – such that for some a drunken driver who causes a fatal accident commits murder, while for others a cold-blooded gunning-down of a defenceless man in front of his wife and children is not murder but an act of armed struggle or war.

These are the words, and they are countless, where establishing the links between words and the world as we perceive it will be most fraught; where our meanings are most likely to diverge, our separateness emerge. In a sense we know this. In so far as we acknowledge it once it is pointed out. But we do not act on it. We fail to see the limitations it imposes on our effective use of language: limitations on the extent to which we can reasonably expect our various meanings to converge.

Difficulties in coming to understand what each other has in their heads arise, not only because the meanings of words are 'various in the Minds of different Men' but also, as Locke points out, one man's 'complex *Idea* seldom agrees with anothers, and often differs from his own, from that which he had yesterday, or will have tomorrow' (III, IX, 6).

If a single individual can differ from day to day, from mood to mood, even from himself, how could convergence with another ever really be straightforward?

Locke's concern to bring the double secret reference out into the open sprang from his conviction that our efforts to communicate are more circumscribed than we often realise. These tacit assumptions are double-edged – hiding from us the extent to which we are cut off, separate from other people, yet at the same time, essential if we are to communicate at all.

Both assumptions, both 'secret references' conceal complexity behind a mask of simplicity. The first invites us to forget that we can never know for certain what our words stand as marks for in another's head; that speaker and hearer meanings are always separate, however similar. The second fosters the illusion that the relation of words for each of us to the world of our experience is more direct, less mind-dependent than it could ever possibly be.

Locke provides no solution because recognising the problem is the only solution. He does succeed, though, in forcing us to see that understanding one another is a difficult enterprise, requiring us to come together from sometimes very different vantage points with no guarantee of success. Forcing us to see that language allows for only a rough and ready sort of communication, that the best we can hope for is close convergence of our separate meanings.

Learning to communicate better means learning to converge more closely more often. And not being too surprised if nevertheless from time to time we fail.

7
Convergence

If we follow through the implications of Locke's double secret reference we arrive at a fresh perspective on understanding and being understood. Once we accept that the meanings of words are necessarily vague and necessarily variable in the minds of different individuals, then it is easy to see how communication can be double-edged. It need not be a problem, but it *can* be one of the worst problems we ever face.

Communicating need not be a problem on those occasions when what we mean by what we say, and what someone else understands by what they hear are the same or very similar. On these occasions, our part-private/part-public meanings vary in the same direction, we 'speak the same language', our meanings CONVERGE.

In many mundane, everyday situations convergence presents few problems. If I ask for a 'pen' and you bring me what I have in mind I can reasonably assume that for all practical purposes, the 'ideas and such' you have in your mind for 'pen' are sufficiently similar to mine for us to understand each other. In addition I can assume that the way I phrased my request, 'Do you think you could get me a pen' or, 'Do you mind getting me a pen', or whatever, were interpreted in a way sufficiently close to what I intended for language to have worked easily and successfully.

It is not always so. On other occasions what I intend and what you understand by the same words may not be so similar; our meanings may to a greater or lesser degree DIVERGE. Not because the words themselves are unfamiliar to either of us, but because in interpreting them, we may bring different facets of their meanings to the fore.

This can happen even in quite simple, everyday cases. You say 'I'm tired' and what you mean and what your partner understands may converge quite straightforwardly: 'So am I, let's go to bed'. Or it may not. You are about to go out for the evening: 'I'm tired' for you expresses a purely physical state, whereas from the strands of meaning knotted by 'tired' your partner may draw 'excuse': 'So you don't want to go then'. 'No, that's not what I meant at all'. Meanings have begun to diverge.

One of the most formidable barriers to achieving convergence and minimising divergence is the real difficulty we have in seeing, or perhaps recalling, what Locke strove to make clear: meanings do not exist independently of minds and minds do not make uniform meanings.

My words, when I say them, in 'their primary or immediate signification stand for nothing but *Ideas*' in my head, while these same words of mine when you hear them stand for *Ideas* in your head.

Meanings are mind-dependent.

The consequence of meanings not existing independently of minds is that for any utterance there will always be at the very least two meanings: a meaning for the speaker – the 'terrain' the words in their conventional patterns represent for him – and a meaning for the hearer – what he understands by the speaker's words.

Two meanings for the same string of words, speaker's and hearer's, mine and yours. Perhaps very similar, perhaps very different. Neither on any account *the* meaning.

The fresh perspective that emerges from Locke's view is that the task we face when trying to understand one another is essentially the task of trying to get our separate meanings to converge.

It seems obvious once we become aware of it. Yet we can find it exceptionally hard to take on board that there is no neutral ground, no external, person-independent, mind-independent vantage point from which to pronounce impartially on the 'real' meaning of any particular string of words. So hard that most of the time when we converse, we do not even see that there could be a need to check. As Locke noted: 'Men stand not usually to examine, whether the *Idea* they, and those they discourse with have in their Minds, be the same' (III, II, 4).

Instead they:

think it enough, that they use the Word, as they imagine, in the common Acceptation of that Language; in which case they suppose, that the *Idea*, they make it a Sign of, is precisely the same, to which the Understanding Men of that Country apply that Name. (III, II, 4)

We use words whose meanings are intricate and variable – words such as 'unemployment' and 'obscene', 'comfort' and 'condone', 'sensitive' and 'caring' and 'consensus' and many, many more – in what we, nevertheless, assume to be their 'common Acceptation'. Yet if so many of the words we string together stand for complexes of ideas put together by each of us through 'the Workmanship of the Understanding' without rules, with no real '*Standards* in Nature, whereby Men may rectify and adjust their significations' (III, IX, 7), then we really have very little grounds for expecting ready convergence between what we individually and separately mean.

Locke offers an image which may help us better grasp the nature of such words – words not straightforwardly anchored in our perception of the outer world: they are, he says, as 'knots' binding collections of ideas into 'bundles': And 'Though therefore it be the Mind that makes the Collection, 'tis the Name which is, as it were, the Knot, that ties them fast together' (III, V, 10).

With this image it is easier to see how words, like knots, can unravel or be only loosely tied, how the complexes of ideas, the bundles, can be tangled or confused. This is not, however, at all the same as saying such words are meaningless. Their meanings rather are multi-faceted, such that when we use them, now one, now another face may come into prominence. Like the crystal patterns in a kaleidoscope.

For our part-private, person-dependent meanings to converge when we use words that knot complexes of ideas, both speaker and hearer must have in mind the same face, the same facet, must draw into prominence the same strand from the bundle of ideas bound by the various words in their particular combination.

Difficult to ensure, unless we remain aware of the difficulty and take positive steps to be specific, expand, give examples. Or if we are the hearer: ask, rephrase, clarify. Assume divergence and work hard towards convergence.

What makes achieving convergence between individuals such a formidable task is our lack of awareness of just how difficult it is. We expect to be able to be precise. After all, numbers are precise. Computer languages are precise. Why should we not expect

natural languages to be precise? Why should we not blame today's
teachers or the lowering of standards or general sloppiness when
they are not?

Our mistake is to look for precision where it could not possibly
be found – Locke wrote:

> Though the Names *Glory* and *Gratitude* be the same in every
> Man's mouth, through a whole Country, yet the complex collect-
> ive *Idea*, which everyone thinks on, or intends by that name, is
> apparently very different in Men using the same Language. (III,
> IX, 8)

For 'Glory' and 'Gratitude' we could equally substitute 'fun' or
'fed up', 'management' or 'maladjusted', 'unusual' or 'upstart'.
There is a great deal of quite ordinary language for which close
convergence with others is very difficult to achieve, not because
we are careless, not because we are sloppy, but simply because of
the diverse, multi-faceted nature of the 'assemblages of ideas'
lying behind the language itself.

Once we accept that convergence is necessarily going to be
difficult, then at least we can recognise that we are going to have to
work hard even to approach some degree of mutual understanding. A deeper carelessness or sloppiness in using language lies in
not even trying to lift the barriers.

To an extent we *can* help others understand us: by giving
concrete examples of what we are talking about, by saying the
same things in several different ways, by circumventing language
in some cases through drawing, showing film or photographs. In
the same way we *can* help others make themselves clearer to us by
admitting when we do not understand, by asking questions, by
reformulating their words into ours and testing them out. Not to
try at all is not to care. To be careless.

However hard we try, however much we may want to understand one another, there will aways be a limit on how far we can
achieve convergence, how far we can understand and be understood. Particularly when we use words that knot complexes of
ideas into bundles – words and expressions such as 'unemployment' or 'maintaining law and order', 'peace' and 'violence', 'style'
and 'selling yourself'; words such as 'care' and 'fair' and 'confidence', 'rights' and 'obligations', 'monitor' and 'argue'. Countless words, combinable into countless phrases, countless utter-

ances. Words – 'knots' – that are often only loosely tied. We never even arrive at a hard and fast, definitive, unchanging meaning for ourselves, let alone one we share with others. Rather we add new strands, new ideas, new facets along with new experience, while other strands become obsolete and fall away.

We all do this, of course, but we do not all do it at the same pace with the same words and expressions. Though we influence one another – language never loses its 'we' side – we nevertheless 'knot' separate 'bundles' with words. Making it almost inevitable that 'the signification of the name' – the meaning of the word – 'that stands for such voluntary Collections, should be often various in the Minds of different Men' (III, IX, 7). Making precision, making close convergence between the meaning intended by a speaker and the meaning arrived at by a hearer ineluctably difficult to achieve, however hard we try.

If we do not try hard enough, it may be because Locke's first 'secret reference' is so deeply ingrained, because we remain so blithely unaware of the tacit assumption that underpins the workings of language – the belief that the words that stand 'as marks' for ideas in my mind stand for the same or similar ideas in your mind. Once we lose sight of the extraordinary tacit assumption that makes communication possible at all, it is only too easy to forget the extent of possible divergence, the degree of possible difference between meanings for ourselves and meanings for others.

8
Convergence and Clarity

If understanding what is meant is essentially a struggle for convergence against the forces of divergence, this has significant implications for clarity – how far we can be clear, whether in some cases it is possible to be clear at all.

The problem is particularly acute when we use words for which there is no 'settled standard . . . in Nature . . . to rectify and adjust their significations by'. What we say can seem clear enough to us in our minds. We may think we know what we are talking about or that it must be obvious what we mean. But we have no fixed standard against which to measure our clarity – or lack of it.

Sometimes writers produce sentences, even whole texts, in which almost all the words stand for complexes of ideas with no 'settled standard . . . in Nature . . . to rectify and adjust their significations by', ideas manufactured by 'the Workmanship of the Understanding'. Speakers may do the same, expounding in a style that rarely touches ground.

Just one example of such prose: an article in a photographic magazine contained a discussion based on Gramsci, of 'the role of photographic imagery in generating active consent to an idea of "Britain".' Included was this sentence: 'It is this slippage between the points of preferred resonance and their popular appropriation which, on the terrain of consent itself, provides both the points of resistance and the points of negotiation'.

'Slippage', 'point of preferred resonance', 'popular appropriation', 'terrain', 'consent', 'points of resistance', 'points of negotiation' – all words and phrases standing for complexes of ideas manufactured by the writer and each individual reader in their own minds through 'the Workmanship of the Understanding'. A sentence within an article largely composed of sentences dominated by this type of word.

It is tempting to claim that such language, unqualified by concrete examples, could never be clear, that assembling such

50

strings of phrases, none of which are rapidly relatable to well-defined 'terrain', sets up an absolute barrier to convergence.

This would not, however, be entirely true. A reader familiar with Gramsci, for instance, may judge the language to be clearer than one who was not. A reader who had discussed with the writer what he was trying to say in his article may likewise find his prose less obscure than we who have had no such preparation.

The difficulty about making generalisations about clarity is that no language is inherently clear or inherently opaque. No language is equally intelligible or equally obscure to all speakers and hearers. Clarity is relative.

Nevertheless, speaking or writing in language dominated by words standing for complexes of ideas with no 'settled standard . . . in Nature . . . to rectify and adjust their significations by' considerably reduces the chances of close convergence with hearers or readers. Particularly when the language is broadcast or published, making it available to be interpreted by a wide and disparate audience approaching from widely-disparate perspectives. Though no language is equally clear or equally obscure to everyone, some types of language are still more likely than others to be readily understood.

Plain English campaigners, both in the UK and the United States, are adept at unearthing examples of language pushed to the bounds of intelligibility. Launched in 1979 by Chrissie Maher and Martin Cutts, the British Plain English Campaign issues annual Golden Bull Awards for really startling cases of impenetrable prose. This was one of the winners: a letter from a Department of Health and Social Security Chief Insurance Officer:

As insurance officer I have decided to review the decision dated 19.9.83 for the following reasons: that by its decision of 31.1.84 the medical board varied the assessment of disablement resulting from the relevant loss of faculty and this constitutes a revision of a decision on a special question.

My revised decision is as follows: A disablement gratuity of £21.50 based on an assessment of 3% per week from 8.6.83 to 22.11.83 and £11.12 per week from 23.11.83 to 6.12.83 based upon an assessment of 20% for the period 8.6.83 to 1.12.83 and a disablement gratuity of £52.75 based upon an assessment of 3% from 2.12.83 to 1.6.84 are awarded for the same accident for

which a disablement gratuity of £21.50 based upon an assessment of . . .

Maher and Cutts, 1986: 12

And so it goes on.

Reading such impenetrable prose it is hard to take on board that
one of its meanings, the Chief Insurance Officer's meaning, the
writer's meaning, was not itself obscure. In his mind 'relevant loss
of faculty', 'decision on a special question', 'disablement gratuity
based on an assessment of x% per week' stood for *Ideas* he was
perfectly familiar with, knowing as he did how the disablement
compensation system works.

The problem arose because Locke's first secret reference had
been completely overlooked. The Chief Insurance Officer assumed
his words, which stood for clear enough *Ideas* for him, who knew
the system, must stand for equally clear *Ideas* for his reader, the
recipient of the letter – an ordinary member of the public who did
not.

He did not see, apparently, that there was not one but at least
two meanings for the words of his letter – his own meaning, and
his reader's. He does not appear to have asked himself whether his
reader's meaning could reasonably be expected to converge upon
his own, given that his reader was not familiar with the disablement compensation system in the way he was. He did not see the
need to put himself in his reader's place, to expand, to explain, to
imagine how his words would strike someone who did not know
what he knew. He was careless. Perhaps he did not care.

Though such cases of writer indifference to reader understanding continue to crop up, the Plain English Campaigns have,
nevertheless, had some effect in the public sector. Since 1982 in
Britain, for instance, 21 300 government forms have been completely revised in an effort to increase convergence between the
meaning of the questions for those asking, and the way they are
understood by those filling in the answers. In the United States
President Carter signed an Executive Order in 1978 requiring
regulations to be written in plain English. The result has been a
steady attack on gobbledegook in many States.

Once the will is there, revising official forms, though mind-
stretching and time-consuming, is not in the end such a difficult
task, providing no one has a vested interest in forms remaining
obscure. If they have been difficult to understand in the past, this

is largely because the writers were insufficiently alert to the possible divergence between what they intended by a question and what a reader might understand.

It is when the will is not there that problems with achieving clarity really arise. Not all speakers and writers want to be clear. Politicians, for instance, often do not. Nor sometimes do trade union and management negotiators or government officials trying to evade difficult issues. Ironically, one of the reasons they are able to avoid plain speaking is because in a sense language allows them to. If they stick largely to language dominated by words standing for complexes of ideas with no 'settled standard . . . in Nature . . . to rectify and adjust their significations by', then they cannot easily be pinned down.

Sir Humphrey Appleby, the fictitious high-ranking civil servant in the British television series *Yes, Minister* is a past master at using language to avoid clarity at all costs: the following is an extract from the diary of Jim Hacker, his unfortunate minister:

'If I might suggest we be realistic about this . . . ', he began.
I interrupted. 'By realistic, do you mean drop the whole scheme?'
'No!' he replied vehemently. 'Certainly not! But perhaps a pause to regroup, a lull in which we reassess the position and discuss alternative strategies, a space of time for mature reflection and deliberation . . . '
I interrupted again. 'Yes, you mean drop the whole scheme.'
Lynn and Jay, 1983: 27

In a more serious vein, George Orwell, in *Politics and the English Language*, attacked what he saw as the 'decline' of English, particularly the ways issues were fudged or evaded by language that rarely touched ground:

This mixture of vagueness and sheer incompetence is the most marked characteristic of modern English prose, and especially of any kind of political writing. As soon as certain topics are raised, the concrete melts into the abstract and no-one seems able to think of turns of speech that are not hackneyed.

Yet being able to use language in a way that leaves our meaning suspended in the mists of vagueness and uncertainty can on occasion be a valuable resource. We can gloss over sensitive issues by remaining in the realms of the general and abstract, we can avoid head-on clashes, get out of embarrassing situations. Vagueness in its right place can sometimes be a virtue.

Sticking to language only loosely linked to any very precise 'terrain' allows us to speak when silence would be inappropriate, though there really is nothing to say. More insidious, however, is when vagueness and obscurity are used wilfully to cloak unpalatable truths. The National Council of Teachers of English in the United States has a Committee of Public Doublespeak which has been making Doublespeak Awards since 1974. Orwell would no doubt have approved. The 1984 winner was a US State Department official with a remark made after the invasion of Grenada when US and Caribbean occupation forces arrested an estimated 1100 Grenadians and others suspected or accused of opposing the invasion. The official denied that US forces were making arrests. 'We are detaining people,' he said. 'They should be described as detainees'.

The State Department also announced 'that it will no longer use the word "killing" in its official reports on the status of human rights around the world. Instead the word "killing" will be replaced by the phrase "Unlawful and arbitrary deprivation of life" (Dayananda, 1986: 15).

Replacing one type of expression, 'killing', with another type, 'unlawful and arbitrary deprivation of life', in official reports is a deliberate attempt to manipulate readers' understanding. 'Killing' is a 'knot' binding a complex of *Ideas* relating to a fairly specific 'terrain': 'killing' is a physical act carried out in the physical world. 'Unlawful and arbitrary deprivation of life' is a combination of 'knots', each binding a wide-ranging complex of *Ideas*, none with any 'settled standard . . . in Nature . . . to rectify and adjust their significations by'.

Readers have to struggle with 'unlawful and arbitrary deprivation of life' to see that it in fact relates to physical acts in the physical world. They have to remain particularly alert if they are to converge with the writer using such language deliberately to make convergence difficult.

This report in the *Guardian* newspaper (10 April 1986) provides another illustration:

A new word is about to enter your life – pico-wave. It's the food and nuclear industries' way of avoiding the word 'radiation' once the Government has given permission, as expected, for the sale of food treated with small doses of gamma rays to increase shelf-life. The plan is for labels saying: 'This food has been pico-waved' and picking up the now acceptable echo of 'microwave.'

If 'pico-wave' does enter our life, it will not be because its inventors have been concerned to find a term that would allow ready convergence between writers using it and consumers reading it on food labels. The prime concern appears to have been to devise an expression that would *not* bind strands, *Ideas*, associated with 'radiation'. The result is a knot that would probably for most people remain only loosely tied, a term they might become used to seeing, would feel that understood vaguely 'some kind of process', 'something they do to food', but would be hazy as to more precise 'terrain'.

*   *   *

The ability we have to hear words, read words, recognise words we only vaguely understand, extends also to the language we produce, to speaking and writing. Sometimes speakers and writers themselves do not know with any clarity what it is they are trying to say. Being pressed to explain, they often find vagueness and indeterminacy surrounding the bundles of ideas their own words have knotted for them.

Unfortunately language allows us to speak and write without necessarily knowing more than vaguely what we are talking about. Part of the reason may lie in a characteristic of language A. N. Whitehead once noted: 'Language,' he wrote 'foists on us exact concepts as though they represented the immediate deliverances of experience' (Whitehead, 1917: 110).

Words and phrases can foist on us trim, tidy concepts, illmatching the messiness, the diversity of people's actual understanding of the world in which they live.

Having words to use can lure us into believing we understand the world better than we can. It can give us an illusion of clarity, allowing us to think that just because we use words and expressions in appropriate combinations we necessarily have a clear idea of the 'terrain' our words are related to.

Words can trip all too easily sometimes from a writer's pen or a speaker's lips. In the Gramsci article, 'generating consent', for instance, is easy enough to write. But who consents? How do we know they consent, whoever they are? Sometimes having a word, a 'knot', 'consent', binding ideas into a convenient bundle, can give a false impression of order and uniformity.

The effort of trying to achieve convergence can expose that false impression for what it is – an often involuntary abuse of language. We have appeared to know because we have used appropriate words, but when we look, 'the words are without clear and distinct *Ideas*', 'signs without anything signified' (Locke, III, X, 2). A using of words that Locke listed high among his abuses of language.

Often the abuse is accidental, but sometimes it is more deliberate. Locke's indignation was particularly stirred by those 'all-knowing doctors' who:

> aiming at Glory and Esteem . . . found this a good Expedient to cover their Ignorance with a curious and unexplicable Web of perplexed Words, and procure to themselves the admiration of others, by unintelligible Terms, the apter to produce wonder, because they could not be understood:' (III, X, 8)

Sometimes we use words to impress, vague about what we mean but confident we will not be challenged. Unless we know someone well, we rarely ask them what exactly they are talking about. We accept their 'unexplicable Web of perplexed Words', thinking we should understand, not knowing that they who speak or write are as vague and uncertain as ourselves.

There are people too who get carried away by the sound of words – words whose ring is the ring of importance – they can so resonate to the sound of their own music that they may easily forget to ask themselves what they have in mind, let alone what others may be understanding.

We have all at one time or another been carried away by the sound of words. Logan Pearsall Smith picked up our gullibility:

> 'Self-determination', one of them insisted.
> 'Arbitration!' cried another.
> 'Cooperation?' suggested the mildest of the party.
> 'Confiscation!' answered an uncomprising female.

I too became slightly intoxicated by the sound of these vocables. And were they not a cure for all our ills? 'Inebriation!' I chimed in. 'Inundation, Afforestation, Flagellation, Transsubstantiation, Co-education!'

Pearsall Smith, 1933: 81

A participant at a computer conference too found himself overwhelmed by words: 'Speakers at these sorts of functions don't discuss, they "share perspectives with you". A perspective is an idea packed out with abstract nouns until it stretches into infinity' (Bidmead, 1986).

The sounds of words, unless we are vigilant, may act as powerful barriers, not only to a convergence of meanings, but also to our understanding our own meanings. Unless we question both ourselves and others about what we have in mind. George Orwell, like Locke, attacked our capacity to repeat words and expressions mindlessly:

> letting the ready-made phrases come crowding in. They will construct your sentences for you – even think your thoughts for you, to a certain extent – and at need they will perform the important service of partially concealing your meaning even from yourself.
>
> G. Orwell, *Politics and the English Language*

Hugo Young gave an example of what Orwell may have had in mind: he was commenting on a speech by a political leader on the theme of 'patriotism':

> Patriotism, it turned out, was just about anything you found it convenient to say it was.
>
> Thus 'ours is a patriotism of production', he said, 'a patriotism of pride in care, a patriotism of jobs and justice.' It is also 'a confident and generous patriotism of freedom and fairness'; and, needless to say, 'a patriotism of today and tomorrow.'
>
> The striking characteristic of these phrases is their complete vapidity, and the proof of it is the ease with which all the words can be transposed without either any loss or any accrual of cogency.
>
> Young, 1986

We can get carried away with words, knot into our bundle only a few loose strands, speak when we have nothing to say, talk of what we ill-understand. The barriers to convergence upon shared meanings are ranged high and deep. They can, to an extent, be overcome. But only by pressing, probing, questioning what it is we and others have in mind.

9

Taking Time to Understand

The various barriers to convergence are not equally significant all of the time. Though language is based on a tacit communal conspiracy whereby we assume, individually, that we mean broadly the same by the same words – Locke's first 'secret reference' – that conspiracy is nevertheless sustained by our experience that *some* of the time we do. More or less. If we ask for 'coffee' at the end of a meal, we are unlikely to get tea. Though if we are not more specific – black, white, milk, cream, sugar, Turkish, cappucino – we may still not succeed in getting precisely the coffee we want.

This is not to say that sometimes it does not take time to arrive at something like common meanings. Time and will, sensitivity and judgement.

If, for instance, over our coffee we ask the friend we have been eating with: 'Will you do me a favour?', the likelihood of our meaning as speaker converging with his meaning as hearer is already lower than when we asked for the coffee. Coffee is part of the physical world. Coffee can be seen and tasted as well as talked about. Coffee too is the expected ending to a meal in our culture. So even if we do not ask, someone else is likely to ask us if we want some. Coffee is generally easy to talk about.

Less so 'favour'. For when we say: 'Will you do me a favour?' for us as speaker the 'favour' is quite specific: we want something. We want to borrow £100 or need a babysitter. For the friend we ask, however, the 'favour' hangs in the air unspecified, 'something he wants from me' possibly accompanied by a prediction: 'I bet he want to borrow the ladder again!'

'Favour' is one of those words whose meaning, manufactured by the mind, has no 'settled standard . . . to rectify and adjust its signification by'. 'Favour' is a knot binding a complex of ideas, its

59

special characteristic the striking initial asymmetry between the meaning the speaker has in mind and the meaning the hearer has in mind. In understanding such words the hearer needs to hang fire, await developments. At the outset he can pick out only one or two strands from the bundle of ideas knotted by 'favour'. Only partly understand.

This type of asymmetry, when a speaker has a specific meaning in mind which the hearer can only partly understand is more widespread than is generally recognised in our ordinary day-to-day language. Take something as commonplace as the use of 'a', the so-called indefinite article. If I say: 'I read a short story last night', my using 'a' is not a sign that my meaning is indefinite, that *I* do not know what story I read. The indefiniteness lies with you, the hearer. You do not know which story I read, and I know that you do not know. My using 'a' marks an indefiniteness that is asymmetrical, with you, the hearer, hanging fire, not yet knowing what I know. This is a case of the grammar of English encoding a distinction between a speaker's own knowledge and his knowledge – or rather belief, for he may be mistaken – about what his hearer knows.

Similarly, in the case of our favour, before the request is made, before the specific nature of the favour is revealed, we would be wrong to suppose that we and our friend, speaker and hearer, mean more or less the same by the same words. Once we ask for the particular favour, however, then our speaker and hearer meanings may well come together. If we say: 'Will you lend me £100?', then the meaning of 'favour' for both of us may converge on the loan of £100, our friend no longer hanging fire.

We are not always so direct. Suppose we still do not say what it is that we want. Some words can be difficult to say, our pride getting in the way, the barriers to convergence lying in ourselves and our reluctance to reveal ourselves rather than any limitations in language. 'Things have been a bit difficult lately', we venture, still with our hope of £100 in mind, though not yet broached. In that case 'favour' for our friend will remain unspecified as he continues to hang fire, waiting for more information before it becomes clear which strands from the bundle of ideas knotted by 'favour' will combine most appropriately with what he knows of us.

If we are too indirect he may easily hare off on quite a different tack, depending on how well he knows our situation. He may interpret 'Things have been a bit difficult lately' as referring to rocky relationships, for instance, invent his own hearer meaning for this particular use of 'favour', understand it as a request to intervene in a row, to mend fences or act as an arbiter.

With this type of language in which words are not readily anchored in the external world, convergence of meanings between speaker and hearer, if it is to be achieved, can take time. It may need questioning or involve abandoning false starts, only eventually and with difficulty picking up the right trail.

Nor can it be guaranteed. If, for instance, I first ask for a 'favour', then I say 'I need £100', I have increased the likelihood of my friend interpreting my statement: 'I need £100' as a request for a loan. Whereas if I say without the preamble of asking for a favour: 'I need £100', still having in mind 'Will you lend me £100?', the likelihood of our speaker and hearer meanings immediately converging is reduced. Particularly if he thinks I know that he is broke. If he does not see himself as a possible lender, since he is broke, he is considerably less likely to interpret 'I need £100' as a request directed at him. Unless he is a particularly self-sacrificing friend . . . Unless . . . Unless . . .

So many possibilities. If I say this, he may understand that, unless I add the other. For speakers and hearers to come to mean the same by the same words may depend on numerous factors – including how much they want to understand.

This capacity we have to hang fire, to understand partly, to keep our hearer meaning 'suspended' until we get more information is an important factor when it comes to understanding how we understand one another. It can help us overcome some of the limitations of language some of the time.

The more we are alert to the dangers of diverging meanings, the more likely we are to see the need to adjust our original interpretations, more likely to achieve convergence in the end, more likely to avoid at least some misunderstanding.

Sometimes divergent meanings are recognised almost immediately and openly corrected. Overheard in a library tea-room at about 4.30 in the afternoon was this snippet of miscommunication:

He: How long have you been here?
She: About two minutes. Just before you came in.
He: I've been here since twelve o'clock.
She: Oh, I see. I thought you meant *here*.

His speaker's meaning for 'here' in the original question as 'in the Library' did not, it becomes apparent, converge with her hearer's meaning of 'in the tea-room'. Thus the question she answers turns out to be a different question to the one he asked. As soon as he says he has been 'here' since twelve o'clock, however, the divergence becomes obvious to her – she assumes he cannot have been in the tea-room for $4\frac{1}{2}$ hours, so she will have to adjust her meaning for his use of 'here'. In so doing she is explicit about her misunderstanding: 'I thought you meant *here*', her speaker meaning for 'here' now 'in the tea-room' and his new hearer meaning too – provided he interprets her misunderstanding successfully.

Though this is a case of divergence brought out into the open, only too often we let it go. Too polite to press. Or we do not care enough. Satisfied to settle for understanding vaguely.

Vaguely understanding, partly understanding, limited convergence. This is the stuff of much so-called communication, the compromise we accept though we rarely acknowledge it to one another. Sometimes we do not like to ask. A woman who had had a miscarriage reported being told by the doctor attending her that it would be better if she did not see her baby. 'The baby would be too macerated – I wouldn't be able to know its sex. I didn't know what the word "macerated" meant, I thought it was like "lacerated". I looked it up later – it means "wasted away".'

Mike, one of the boys who took part in Howard Gannaway's research on the way children make sense of school recalled some of his earlier uncertainties:

When we first came to this school, and they told us what subjects we were going to do . . . I was really baffled because I didn't know what Classics was. I had no idea, and at one stage I thought it was classical music . . . They didn't tell you what you were going to do. It was just put on a plate.

Gannaway, 1976: 58

Another example of the way private uncertainty can lead to unexposed confusion. Unexposed because when in those early days Mike's teachers talked of doing Classics, they did not know, if he sat quietly and did not ask or look puzzled, that he was understanding 'classical music' or not understanding at all. We easily assume understanding in others although we know full well that we ourselves do not necessarily admit when we do not understand.

Even when people use the same words as one another with apparent confidence, words they are both familiar with, there is still no guarantee of close convergence. Take this extract from a recorded interview between two academics and a woman who had applied to read English as a mature student at the University of London:

Interviewer: And you're fairly well-equipped in present day reading . . . beginning of this century –
Interviewee: Um . . . well I – I don't know that I'd go as far as to say that I was fairly well-equipped . . . I mean I've read generally but not with any purpose in mind you know.

Svartvik and Quirk, 1980: 755

Both the interviewer and the prospective student use the same expression in this extract: 'fairly well-equipped' – 'fairly well-equipped in present day reading'. But how far can we suppose their speaker and hearer meanings for the expression converge? How far do they actually understand one another?

We cannot know. But we can speculate: if pressed would the interviewer have been able to supply a ready set of criteria for what constitutes 'fairly well-equipped' in present day reading? Number of novels, poems, plays read, degree of familiarity, penetration, level of critical analysis?

Or was 'fairly well-equipped' a loose knot for him: 'fairly well-equipped in present day reading' being equivalent to something like 'has read an unspecified amount and has something perceptive to say about what she has read'?

If the latter were nearer the truth – certainly the overall tenor of the interview is vague and disjointed – then how would this affect the likelihood of his meaning as speaker and her meaning as hearer closely converging?

In her response the prospective student picks up the interviewer's words, disclaiming what he suggests. But is she disclaiming the same thing as he was suggesting? Would this even be possible if he was vague and imprecise about what 'fairly well-equipped in present day reading' meant for him in the first place?

It is a strange truth about language that she would not need to know at all clearly what he meant in order to disclaim it. Part of knowing a language is mastery of grammatical form and patterns. We know the forms of words that will allow us to deny something or to ask a question.

Her 'I don't know that I'd go as far as to say that' is a form of
words that allows her to modify whatever assumption the speaker
appears to have been making about her. She can use the form of
words with only the vaguest grasp of the nature of that assumption.

Thus her speaker meaning for 'fairly well-equipped' in her
response to the interviewer could represent a hanging fire; it could
be as vague as: 'whatever *you* meant by fairly well-equipped'. She
could, by awaiting developments, be playing safe. From the
bundle of ideas knotted for her by 'well-equipped' she may have
picked out, for example, the notion of competence: he thinks I
have some unspecified level of competence. I don't know what
level that is, but if it is too high he might start asking me difficult
questions. So it is probably safer if I lower his expectations – whatever they may be.

All this is speculation. But speculation of a kind that shows how
conversations can be carried on with only partial understanding,
limited convergence. How far the interviewer's meaning actually
diverged from that of the prospective student did not come out
into the open as this particular interview progressed. Unremarked
or unresolved divergence is more common than we think.

In a case like this, a formal interview, it is often easier for an
interviewer than an interviewee to press and probe, question and
check, attempt to increase convergence. He might have asked:
have you read Lawrence and Forster, Golding and Greene, Roth
and Rubens, Lodge and Bradbury? Examples are often assets to
convergence. He could have helped her begin to arrive at some
idea, however shadowy, of the 'terrain' he had in mind for 'fairly
well-equipped in present day reading.' But interviews are rather
special language games where convergence of meanings may
matter less than making the right impression, the right noises.

Language allows us to make the right noises. Making it difficult
for us to know sometimes whether we are understanding one
another. 'Some people do not quite understand but they don't
want the other person to know that they are as dumb as they are,
so that they pretend that they understand', the head of an
engineering firm said in an interview with Leah Hertz. She had
been widowed at 58 and had taken over the firm without any
engineering experience at all:

I said to everybody, 'I do not know anything, you have an ignorant person here, but I want to learn so please repeat it'. And sometimes they would get sick of repeating it and I would say, 'Either you are not explaining it right or my brain is not thinking it right. Explain it again,' and they knocked themselves out. If you act too smart they think, 'Smart aleck'. But if you say to a man or a woman, 'I need help. I want to learn. Can you help me?' they knock you down trying to help you.

Hertz, 1986: 14

Most of the time we do not make such an effort. We do not probe, sometimes because we cannot for fear of offending, or of embarrassing by showing up ignorance or uncertainty.

So we end up sometimes having conversations we are not sure we understand. Only we do not like to say for fear of revealing the emperor in all his nakedness.

10

Private Uncertainty, Public Confusion

We do not always understand others, but we usually assume that they know what they are talking about. Or at least, we assume they believe they do.

At the same time, however, we know from our own experience that we often use language we only partly understand. Indeed, it is one of the more intriguing sides of speaking a language that we can be familiar with particular words and phrases, know how they sound when said, how they look when written down, even know broadly what area of experience they are usually associated with yet be unable to link them to any specific 'terrain'. Even more intriguing, perhaps, is the way we can produce perfectly well-formed sentences using these words we ill-understand.

Much of the time it hardly matters that we can speak or write without entirely knowing what we mean. Usually we manage to keep our uncertainties private and only the individuals involved need be affected.

Richard Boston once revealed publicly some of the words he found most stubborn: 'There are certain words that, however often I look them up in the dictionary, I still have no idea what they mean when I next bump into them. Ontological, for example, Teleology. Rebarbative. Reification' (Boston, 1986).

Not knowing what they mean would not, however, prevent him from producing a sentence such as 'That kind of teleology assumes an ontological commitment I find rebarbative,' even if he did not have much idea what his speaker meaning was. He could do it because he knows the forms and patterns of English – which is not, of course, to say he would.

Others might though, and sometimes do. Most of us have had that feeling of words falling around us like snow, soft, elusive and bewildering, sounds without sense, words adrift from their 'terrain'.

66

When private uncertainty remains within the private domain, its ill-effects can be limited. But when, in public, words come adrift from a specifiable 'terrain', the consequences can be more serious. In particular, when these are words used by political leaders, administrators, decision-makers devising policies affecting people's lives.

One striking example of such a word with far-reaching implications emerged from research into the field of social work carried out mainly in Scotland by Stuart Rees and Alison Wallace. In the course of talking to social workers, clients, administrators and others, they found widespread use of the term 'evaluation'. It seemed that as government was becoming more cost-conscious, the need to 'evaluate' activities carried out in the public sector was becoming widely-accepted.

When Rees and Wallace discussed evaluation with a number of top administrators, however, these Directors of Social Work 'admitted to difficulty in saying what they meant by evaluation. It was a struggle for them to relate "evaluation" to specific activities'.

When asked to give illustrations of what they understood by evaluation only the most general ideas emerged:

> Evaluation was sometimes synonymous with management . . . Secondly, evaluation was related to activities concerned with accountability . . . The third concern was with the constant business of assessing and being assessed. The directors admitted that to their minds the processes of everyday work and life involved evaluation. In this respect evaluation was implicit seldom explicit, inherent yet invisible, governing activities but not according to criteria which were acknowledged openly.
> Rees and Wallace, 1982: 12–13

Though they had difficulty in pinning down what they understood by evaluation, it did not follow that in any straightforward way these Directors of Social Work did not understand the meaning of the word. As far as they were concerned, no doubt, they did. They assented to the desirability of 'evaluation' being carried out, the word knotting for them in their different ways some general notions – management, accountability, assessment – of what areas broadly might be involved.

Yet in applying these general notions specifically to their own field, the public domain for which they were responsible as decision-makers, none of them seemed able to say at all clearly what anyone might actually *do* in order to evaluate the activities of social workers.

Recall A. N. Whitehead's warning: 'Language . . . foists on us exact concepts as though they represented the immediate deliverances of experience'.

In this instance the *word* 'evaluation' may have given, not only the Directors, but also their political masters – MPs, councillors – the illusion of a trim and tidy concept of 'evaluation', far removed from the messy and difficult problems of actually trying to evaluate the diverse, subjective, inexhaustably varied field of day-to-day social work with real people and real problems.

Perhaps this should not have been surprising. As Rees and Wallace remark on the very plausibility of evaluating social work: 'Evaluation requires agreement about the nature of social work and some discussion of its diverse objectives, a task which has some resemblance to wading through a quagmire' (Rees and Wallace, 1982: 6).

Worthwhile evaluation in almost any domain would undoubtedly require considerable ground-clearing – the work of Locke's 'Under-Labourer . . . removing some of the Rubbish, that lies in the way to Knowledge'. It would require making explicit judgements and values that had been implicit, arriving after considerable time and hard thought at some measure of agreement as to which particular activities should be evaluated and how. We rarely make such an effort. Often too when politicians, pressure groups, public bodies of all sorts call for 'evaluation', 'assessment', making people 'accountable', they show little evidence of knowing what such demands would actually involve in practice. Words with the right ring often appear to be enough.

Talk about evaluating, like accountability, has the right ring to it – it sounds like something administrators should be doing or politicians should be insisting upon. The reality is, however, that 'evaluation' belongs to a class of particularly difficult and complex words which require effort to link them to a firm 'terrain'. Any serious discussion of the 'terrain' 'evaluation' points to, throws up other complex terms such as 'standards', 'goals', 'quality', 'priorities', 'monitoring' – all 'knots' containing 'knots' within 'knots', none of them easy to untie.

Not surprisingly, Rees and Wallace also found a good deal of uncertainty surrounding one of the 'knots' within the 'evaluation knot': the problem term this time was 'standards': 'Although there seemed to be agreement that there existed in the various agencies . . . an unspoken expectation that standards were to be maintained, nobody was terribly clear as to what these standards might be' (Rees and Wallace, 1982: 92).

'Standards' is another difficult term, not least because maintaining them is so patently something we cannot reasonably be against. Politicians often wish to go further and insist that standards be laid down, imposed from outside. Not so difficult when we are talking about physical standards – building standards, for instance – much more so when the standards to be maintained are not easily measurable, quantifiable – academic standards, for instance.

The UK Committee of Vice-Chancellors and Principals has a group which deals with academic standards. In the opening sentence of the Foreword to the Committee's 1986 Report, the Chairman, Professor P. A. Reynolds, acknowledged their dilemma, the private uncertainties likely to underlie public confusion: 'Quality and standards are words in constant use. Few stop to think precisely what they mean and many could give no precise definition if they did.' (1986: 3).

For the Academic Standards Group, the most difficult aspect of monitoring standards was 'the measurement of what actually happens to students during their progress from first to final year of a first degree programme, or during their lonely pursuit of research for a higher degree.'

The problem for an outside body trying to assess standards within universities is that: 'The description of the purposes of a course, of its syllabus, of its assessment methods, and of the resources required for it may be admirable, but what actually happens in the lecture-hall, the laboratory or the seminar room may be quite inadequate'.

This particular committee set itself a relatively modest task, not of setting standards, but of trying to identify the procedures by which the universities themselves might: 'increase the degree of validity and reliability of standards, and thus make judgements of quality to some extent less fallible' (1986: 9).

They were not carried away by words with the right ring – 'less fallible' strikes the right note of caution about what they felt could be achieved. In the end they concluded that the most reliable safeguard of standards was not external validation or any other outside control. Rather it was: 'the growth of the teaching institution as a self-critical academic community'.

If 'maintaining standards' is to be more than just a phrase, uncertainly linked to specific 'terrain', individuals within groups have to come to agree among themselves what standards they should aim for and how they should be maintained. This can take time and effort, wrestling, within the constraints of polite discussion, with 'the intolerable burden of meanings'. Only this way are private understandings likely to converge on a 'common acceptation', and even then only for that particular group. Other groups would likewise have to be their own 'Under-Labourers'. Only then is there any real chance of public confusion being diminished.

* * *

As well as presenting us with knots of extraordinary complexity to unpick, language fortunately provides us also with easy routines where private uncertainty and public confusion seem almost to disappear in a miracle of instant and effortless convergence.

Some language routines are common to entire speech communities, some are restricted to small groups, all nevertheless minimise the difficult 'I' side of language, luring us into believing that convergence is easy.

11
Language on Automatic Pilot

'Humankind cannot bear too much reality.'

T. S. Eliot

It is an irony little remarked upon that language used routinely as part of regularly-performed rituals represents language working at its smoothest. When we greet each other, or say goodbye, when we go shopping, say thanks, order coffee at a counter, or a meal in a restaurant, when we introduce ourselves or others or ask the way, we have readily at our disposal a range of phrases that are appropriate: Excuse me, can you tell me the way to King's College Chapel? Two coffees, please. Yes, white. Have you met my sister? That's very kind of you. Thanks.

And we know too without really thinking how it is appropriate to respond: I'm a stranger here, I'm afraid. Yes, it's down there on the right. You can't miss it. Bye. See you later. Take care. Enjoy the play. Pleased to meet you. How long are you down here for?

We understand one another. As speakers and hearers our separate meanings are likely to converge quite closely. We have done it before, many times. Familiar people in familiar situations. Or unfamiliar people, but using familiar words.

The language routines which pervade so much of our everyday life can help hide the problems inherent in talking about the things that are not routine. For the irony is that what we value most in language – creativity, expressiveness, the capacity to move, to convince, to persuade, to reason – allows us to succeed less well in having others understand us than the largely prefabricated phrases we use to say almost the same thing over and over again. Paradoxically, language is at its best when it matters least; at its worst when it matters most.

71

There is a further tension within the human condition, not entirely separate from the public and the private, a tension this time between the innovative and the imitative, between our capacity to be creative, individual, original and our need to be habitual, commonplace, robotic.

We all act as robots sometimes. In the film, *A Thousand Clowns*, Jason Robards Jr indulges in a little subversive mockery by accosting a string of total strangers in the street: 'I'm sorry, I'm so sorry', he says. 'That's quite all right', they replied robotically through their surprise.

A fiction, but a highly plausible fiction. We are all familiar with the 'saying sorry' routine. We have apologised and been apologised to ten thousand times. We have used the same routine on accidentally jostling someone, or on deliberately wounding their pride. It has become part of us so that we can switch it on without necessarily thinking. It can be triggered off without our conscious intervention.

This does not mean though that our routines are always robotic. We can be creative with a familiar routine. Give the accepting apology response: 'That's all right' flatly, tonelessly to show it is not all right at all. Repeat 'Sorry, sorry, sorry' a score of times until we feel quite genuinely forgiven.

Routines, set phrases, clichés, are not invariable, nor are they dispensable. We need them. We need them when silence is inappropriate but we do not know what to say. We need them to conceal embarrassment. We even have set phrases for saying we do not know what to say, at funerals, for instance, where in the United States reportedly 'There's really nothing to say at a time like this', is one of the commonest remarks to be heard (Tannen and Oztek, 1981: 38).

We need them when circumstances throw us together with total strangers. While silence may be appropriate in a doctor's waiting room, or a bus queue, or on a plane, it is not at a party, squashed face to face in a crowded room with a full glass and an empty mind. We need words, ready-made, prefabricated phrases to conceal our disquiet or to allow the moment to pass, or to get started. We need the 'What do you do?' or 'Where are you from?' or the remarks about the decor or the host or the music. If we are lucky the responses will reveal some common interest or attitude, some affinity, so we can set routine aside and move into a more innovative mode. And if we are not, then clichés can often tide us over until we see the opportunity to slip away.

In his book on clichés, Anton Zijderveld argued that a good deal of ordinary, everyday talk is only possible at all: 'if the bulk of it runs off automatically i.e. without much cognition and emotive effort, and with little psychic investment' (Zijderveld, 1979: 57). Behind the heavy prose lies an important observation: one reason we need routines to help us say what is appropriate, react in ways others judge as normal, is that communicating on anything but a superficial level engages the mind and the emotions to an extent it is difficult and tiring to sustain. We cannot do it for too long at a time. We need to be allowed to be robots. Engaging with others, striving hard for convergence, trying to express what we think and feel, struggling to understand their views and feelings about things that matter to them – what some would call 'real' communication – is a difficult and emotionally-draining task. So much so that some people spend much of their time avoiding it.

Humankind, T. S. Eliot reminded us, cannot bear too much reality.

Another more down-to-earth reality most of us face is spending our lives – at work, at home – in the presence of other people. For these conditions to be manageable, survivable, we need to be free to ignore others a certain amount of the time, and for the rest to be able to converse around often repeated topics, using tried and tested phrases – uninnovative, uncreative. In these circumstances, routine expressions, clichés, habitual phrases, all come to our rescue, keep us waving not drowning. Language used not so much to communicate as to sustain some solidarity, nurture a little empathy.

Yet routine, like so many other attributes of language, is double-edged – essential to our survival, it can at the same time prevent us from trying to get through to others when perhaps they need us, hinder us from making any real contact. Relying too much on routine can damage our relationships, blunt our creativity. Once we start hiding behind routines, using them to avoid, rather than simply oil the wheels of contact with others, then we are getting the balance wrong, forever imitating when we could be innovating.

Not that all routines are straightforward. Some are only semi-automatic, 'half-and-half' routines where one side knows exactly

what is wanted, the other not. Consultations with professionals –
doctors or solicitors, for example – can sometimes be like this.
Researchers Webb and Stimson made a study of patients' accounts
of going to the doctor. They observed:

> It is because the doctor regularly and routinely holds consulta-
> tions that he develops a routine and range of strategies that he
> may call upon in his interaction with the patient. The patient is
> not usually as experienced at 'managing' the consultation or in
> 'managing' doctors.
>
> Webb and Stimson, 1976: 116

It may, for instance, be important to a doctor's diagnosis to
establish whether a patient is suffering 'discomfort' or 'pain'. In
this extract from a consultation, recorded by Coulthard and
Ashby, the doctor guides the patient towards 'discomfort':

> *Doctor*: But you don't actually get pain in the shoulder?
> *Patient*: No . . . a pain . . . something that seems to er . . .
> *Doctor*: You find it difficult to describe.
> *Patient*: Yes, Doctor.
> *Doctor*: It's not a true pain in the shoulder . . .
> *Patient*: No . . . not a . . .
> *Doctor*: . . . but a discomfort.
> *Patient*: It opens and shuts sort of business.
> *Doctor*: Yes yes. Would you describe it as a discomfort in your
> shoulder?
> *Patient*: Yes Doctor.
> *Doctor*: Rather than a true pain.
> *Patient*: Yes.
>
> Coulthard and Ashby, 1976: 81

The doctor brushes aside the patient's efforts to specify the
nature of the pain/discomfort – 'It opens and shuts sort of business' – pressing him to assent to one or the other label, even
though the patient cannot know how the doctor sees the distinction, where for him discomfort ends and pain begins. In
exchanges of this asymmetric sort, where the layperson ends up
agreeing with the professional, convergence of meanings is often
more apparent than real.

Such half-and-half routines can be extremely unsatisfactory for patients, though they may appear on the surface to work smoothly. There may be good reasons why they have been developed – GPs, for example, have very little time for each patient so that they need to structure their consultations, elicit relevant information rapidly, if they are to survive at all. Patients, though, can feel shut out by doctors who hide too persistently behind their routines. Though they may not necessarily say anything, they can nevertheless feel the doctor is not really listening, that they are not getting through.

Webb and Stimson comment on their particular all-female patient sample:

> When the doctor dismisses a problem as unimportant or ignores a symptom presented by the patient, the patient's lack of persistence may not necessarily indicate that she too now perceives that problem as insignificant. It is noticeable in many consultations that, just as the dialogue is drawing to a close, the patient makes frequent agreeing sounds as though these are as appropriate as the farewells and thanks that mark the exit. This formal acquiescence, however, is often a guise that falls away once the patient is back in the lay world among friends and relatives.
>
> Webb and Stimson, 1976: 118–19

Some studies of classroom language have highlighted another type of half-and-half or asymmetrical routine characteristic of some types of teacher/pupil talk. Some teachers' language has been found to be composed of little riddles where the pupils have to guess the particular word or phrase the teacher is thinking of.

In this short extract, an English teacher is discussing a poem with the class:

> *Teacher*: Well, I'm going to help you – a word beginning with A.
> *Pupil*: Attitudes.
> *Teacher*: Yes, now answer again using the word 'attitudes'.
>
> Stubbs, 1976: 99

Pupils unable or unwilling to take part in the riddle-routine in learning could find themselves, for quite inappropriate reasons, seriously disadvantaged at school.

Such routines are an example of language seeming easy to one side – the 'insider', the professional – while possibly being quite confusing to the other. Insider and outsider are not necessarily 'speaking the same language', though they may be using the same words.

A great deal easier than half-and-half routines are those fashions of speaking we are familiar with among the various groups we move in. At work, in the pub, playing sport, at home, with friends, with relatives – anywhere where we belong. We come to understand, to participate in gossip, standing jokes, ways of being and ways of speaking. For when we belong, when the conditions are right, convergence can seem easy. We take it for granted until we find ourselves with a group of which we are not a member – a new job, new club, new neighbourhood, and suddenly feel shut out, uncomprehending, lonely.

The same language that can make some people feel they belong can shut others out. Any particular example of language is itself indifferent, a catalyst provoking a response. We respond – feel shut out or brought in from the cold, depending on whether or not we belong. For when we do, familiar language, routine language, can keep us firmly in the fold, help us survive in an otherwise indifferent world.

12
Language Solidarity

In his book *Alone*, explorer Richard Byrd gives a moving account of his rescue from an Antarctic weather base, his rescuers a team of men who had risked their lives to reach him. Reflecting on the experience he recalls being struck by his rescuers' talk when they arrived:

> And I do remember thinking that much of what they said was as meaningless as if it were spoken in an unfamiliar tongue . . .
> [Even though the tongue was English] for they had been together a long time, occupied with common experience, and in their talk they could take a good deal for granted. I was the stranger.
>
> Byrd, 1938: 298–9

We have all, in less extraordinary circumstances, experienced that odd sensation, the *frisson* of the outsider.

Starting a new job, joining a club or society, coming as a stranger to any established group, we have all felt disoriented, shut out by the language used around us, heard familiar-sounding words that, somehow, refused to take on meaning, recognised the words being spoken, with little idea what was being talked about. Our meanings and their meanings not so much diverging or converging as remaining on distinct, parallel lines.

Generally if we are quick and alert, it is not long before understanding begins to dawn, before convergence becomes closer. Sometimes so anxious are we to belong that we even pretend convergence is closer than it is, laugh at the standing jokes before we fully understand.

Anthropologist John Beard Haviland came upon a more intractable problem than we normally face while doing fieldwork in an Indian community in Zinacantan in south-east Mexico. He had gone to some lengths to learn the local language, Tzotzil, yet he was aware that there was much that people said he did not understand. As they chatted and gossiped he felt very much an outsider, shut out, though not unkindly: 'although I could understand people's *words*,' he wrote, 'I could not understand the gossip itself. It took me some time to discover what knowledge and skills I was lacking' (Haviland, 1977: 48).

What he came to see was that learning the sounds, the words and phrases, the conventional patterns of Tzotzil was no more than a preliminary step. What he lacked was the shared experience, the common knowledge of local people – leaders and led, conformers and non-conformers – their history, their generosity or their meanness, their honesty or dishonesty, their virtues and vices, knowledge local people brought to bear on everything they heard and said. Without all this he was in effect suspended between recognising the words yet being able to form no more than a hazy idea of their 'terrain'.

To move out of his state of suspension, to get the conditions for convergence right, Haviland recognised he would have to learn more about what the words were being used to talk about. So he began to compile a 'Who's Who?' of the village, based on lengthy talking sessions with local people. As he learnt more about the loves and loyalties, the quarrels and concerns of this particular community, the villagers slowly began to treat him as an insider, to include him in their talk, to gossip with him – outsider turned insider.

It is hard to remember sometimes that just because people around you are speaking your language, or a language you are familiar with, this does not mean you will necessarily understand what they are talking about. The men who rescued Richard Byrd were using words which were perfectly recognisable. But because they 'had been together a long time, occupied with common experience,' such that 'in their talk they could take a good deal for granted', they did not need to elaborate or explain things to one another.

It is an irony about language we have already remarked that it works most smoothly when it is least necessary, among people who already know to a great extent what they are talking about. In this case it was Byrd, the outsider, who did not understand. He had not shared their particular experience, he had not built up a common way of being with them. Convergence which was effortless for them was close to complete divergence for him.

At the same time many of the ways of speaking developed among groups of friends, colleagues, rivals even, prove transient. Even Byrd's rescuers, once their ordeal was over and they were back in ordinary life would inevitably lose some of their particular closeness, their ease of talking, the capacity to converge with one another almost effortlessly.

'Insider talk' is often a response to a common task or else a crisis, such as that which arose during the first few troubled weeks at the British early morning television company, TV-am, and which resulted after intense politicking in the almost complete break-up of the original team of presenters for the morning show, *Good Morning Britain* – the 'Famous Five' – Michael Parkinson, David Frost, Anna Ford, Angela Rippon, Robert Kee. The programme's first editor Hilary Lawson, wrote:

> In the ensuing whirl of alliance and counter-alliance, the canal, passing as it did directly alongside the building, assumed more and more importance. The metaphor began as in the phrase, 'Who is going to throw whom in the canal?' – an incessant topic of conversation among potential participants. This later developed into a form of canal shorthand as in 'Anna-splash I expect, but maybe all-of-us-splash'
>
> Lawson, 1984

Canal shorthand, we suspect, is long dead and gone at TV-am, though in its day it served a group in their hour of crisis.

Most likely too there are few of the original participants left who would now remember the significance of this classroom exchange recorded in the 1970s by researchers R. Walker and C. Adelman:

> After one boy, Wilson, had finished reading out his rather obviously skimped piece of work [on 'Prisons'], the teacher sighed and said, rather crossly:
>
> *Teacher*: Wilson, we'll have to put you away if you don't change your ways and do your homework. Is that all you've done?
> *Boy*: Strawberries, strawberries. (Laughter)
>
> Walker and Adelman, 1976: 138

This bizarre response was perfectly intelligible to all the participants, even if it would not have been to anyone else. It turned out that one of the teacher's favourite expressions was that too much of the work he saw was: 'Like strawberries – good as far as it goes, but it doesn't last nearly long enough'.

It was an example which crystallised for these particular researchers the different levels of understanding of the same language achievable by insiders to a group compared with outsiders unfamiliar with the 'terrain'. They comment:

> meanings are not simply dictionary labels attached to words which we 'learn'; the words themselves have associations and particular, personal meanings not readily accessible to those outside the immediate experience of the group. As outsiders, when we look at lesson transcripts, what we tend to see is the bare bones of meaning – the universals freely available within our culture – not the full richness of talk, which is what makes a relationship valuable and unique to its participants.
>
> Walker and Adelman, 1976: 139

The words themselves belong within a 'terrain', while the 'terrain' is often private to a group, so that an outsider, though recognising the words, does not understand. As English speakers we are perfectly familiar with the word 'strawberries', in so far as we could give a description that would gain a measure of 'common acceptation' of something in the physical world we would refer to using this word. Furthermore we could all make up sentences in which 'strawberries' appears appropriately. Yet none of this would prevent us reading this transcript without having any idea of the significance of 'strawberries' here. Until we know the conditions that make convergence easy, we remain outsiders, recognising the words but not their 'terrain'.

Some ways of speaking, along with some ways of behaving, are less transient. Some become well established, such that it can be possible to transfer from one office or school or branch of a political party or self-help group to another, elsewhere, yet still find similar patterns, still be able to latch on to the group without undue difficulty.

Alcoholics Anonymous provides a striking example. Researcher David Robinson found, while making a detailed study of AA, that 'AA talk' was well-recognised as such by members: 'I've talked to you,' one said to Robinson, 'like an ordinary person, not doing AA talk like I would to another AA. You get into the way of switching

on to the other. It just becomes automatic' (Robinson, 1979: 74).
  Or another:

> I'm trying to make this sound not like I would talk at an AA
> meeting, 'cos often it comes over a bit different . . . I went to see
> some people, other than AA. That was quite a good evening. It
> was two different worlds again. I went from one to the other. It
> was a straight contrast from AA type talking and general talking
> to ordinary people.
>
> Robinson, 1979: 104

Sometimes, too, people find that particular talk is special, not
because of the content or the style, but the fact that they feel free to
talk as they wish. A woman said of her friend: 'I feel when I'm
with her, I'm totally honest. I can say whatever I want to.
Sometimes I feel there are very few times in my life when I can
really do that' (Johnson and Ariès, 1983: 358).
  Or actress Julie Christie talking about making the film *The Gold
Diggers*, working entirely with women:

> It was an enormous relief being with women. There are all sorts
> of odd things you can do with your own sex which you don't do
> when there's a man around . . . Language, behaviour, every-
> thing was uncensored . . . Because of our common experience,
> we could communicate everything in shorthand and it was
> delightful being able to do that. There was no need for explana-
> tions.
>
> Berlins, 1984

Some special ways of speaking or writing become so well-
established they become part of the identity of a group, their
jargon which others have to master to join. Such jargon may be
known as technical terms if the group are experts belonging to a
respectable academic discipline. Some jargon is more comprehensible than others to outsiders. This extract appeared in *The Times*:

> 'Take bottle the splonk, neves to rouf bar, Mary the rag'.
> Gibberish? Code? Some obscure foreign language? No, a mix-
> ture of back and rhyming slang used by bookmakers to shout
> the odds (take 2-1 the favourite, 7-4 Bar, 8-1 the outsider).

Simple, even logical to those familiar with the jargon; otherwise unintelligible – exactly like some bidding at the bridge table.

Flint, 1986

Part of an article which went on to talk about bridge in a manner quite unintelligible to the non-bridge-playing outsider.

At a different level of abstraction, consider the following passage from a paper by J. Findlay in the journal *Mind*:

We cannot prove the statement which is arrived at by substituting for the variable in the statement form 'We cannot prove the statement which is arrived at by substituting for the variable in the statement form Y the name of the statement form in question' the name of the statement form in question.

Findlay, 1942: 262

Though Findlay states that the aim of his paper is 'to make clearer for the benefit of those who have little taste for the intricacies of mathematical logic, the general significance of Goedel's important logical discoveries' (Findlay, 1942: 259), most of us could probably read his self-embedded sentence over and over again without ever making head or tail of it. Yet according to Polanyi, Bertrand Russell, skilled in the appropriate mathematics and interested in the problems posed by self-referential statements, took in what Findlay had in mind at a single glance.

*   *   *

Fortunately we are nearly all insiders somewhere. That is why language at times can seem easy, because we know the 'terrain', we have shared experiences and expectations with other people, we have beliefs, opinions, skills in common with those we talk to, so that the conditions for convergence are readily satisfied. But as soon as we leave our sheltered, familiar worlds, as soon as we feel the chill of being an outsider descend, the real difficulties inherent in communicating with others make themselves felt again.

The same words may be simple or impossible to understand, allow convergence or create divergence. Understanding cannot be taken for granted even when it seems easy. No words are ever easy in themselves, only easy because the conditions for convergence are right.

Part II
Language, Sense and Emotion

'The limits of language are not the last limits of experience and things inaccessible to language may have their own symbolic devices.'

S. Langer, *Philosophy in a New Key*

13

Seeing Faces

'Words can't exactly describe it.'
Wittgenstein

If we were primarily rational beings, the limitations of language would be less acute. For rational beings communication – convergence between our meaning as speaker and another's as hearer – would be less affected by moods and feelings, whether we were drawn to each other, whether one or other of us was upset or elated, depressed or bored. Rational beings would rely much less than we do on hunches and intuitions, on what we feel or sense but could not put more than grossly into words.

Language is so central to us that we can easily underestimate how much we know and experience independently of words. Tastes, smells, the ambience of a place, the way we feel inside, the moods of other people, the sensations that succeed one another, pain, pleasure, surges of life and energy, the dead weight of apathy or depression.

As a result we too rarely consider the effects of feelings and emotions on our use of language or whether language allows us to express at all adequately what we experience independently of words. Sometimes though we are brought up short:

'I've never tasted mangoes. What do they taste like?' 'Well, they're sort of sweet, they've got quite a distinctive taste'. 'Yes, but what sort of a taste?' 'Well it's sort of perfumy, I suppose'. 'Perfumy? . . . '

'I'm feeling kind of odd today'. 'Are you ill?' 'No, not ill exactly, just sort of funny, my head feels funny'. 'Headache, is it?' 'No, not exactly. Just odd, if feels odd'.

Familiar tastes, sensations sharply-felt yet translatable only clumsily into words.

The purpose of this part of the book is to explore the relation of language to our senses and emotions and to highlight some of the ways in which our use of language is limited by the non-rational sides of ourselves.

To give some idea of just how complex the relationship can be, suppose we start with perhaps the most crucial of our senses: seeing. Throughout our waking hours our eyes feed signals to the brain, signals the brain converts to information about the world around us – recurring similarities, subtle and not so subtle changes.

Some of this information concerns the people we see: their dress, their build, their height, their stance, their faces. Especially their faces. Our eyes provide us with a lot of information about faces. Some we recognise immediately, some are only vaguely familiar, some are the faces of strangers.

All these faces are in essence very similar to one another, particularly if their owners belong to the same race. Each one consists of the same basic set of features in the same configuration. A visitor from another planet, unfamiliar with humans, might well have considerable difficulty in telling them apart.

We, however, have no such difficulty. On the contrary, it seems to us self-evident that individual faces are sufficiently different for us to distinguish them from one another. They look different. Anyone can see that.

Our intuition is supported by researcher in face recognition, Haydn Ellis: 'Most of us can discriminate among an almost infinite number of faces,' he says, 'and we can probably identify several thousands, even if we are unable to provide a name for each one'. He reports Bahrick *et al.* as showing that:

> the vast memory for faces is also durable: people asked to identify photographs of class mates' faces when mixed with other faces displayed a very high success rate 15 years later, and even after a 50-year lapse about three quarters of the faces were correctly classified.
>
> Ellis, 1981: 171

People matter to us as individuals making their separate faces take on a special significance. We learn to 'read' faces, confirming Hogarth's famous dictum: 'The face is the index of the mind'.

Some of us are sensitive to almost imperceptible shifts of expression, a slight tightening of the features, pursing of the lips.

The face, as researchers in the mechanisms of visual perception have less elegantly rephrased it, is an 'important source of sociobiological information'. We often make judgements, assess moods, for instance, by looking at facial expression – 'He's not looking too cheerful today. Must be something the matter' – 'What are you looking so pleased with yourself for?' Sometimes we assess character, even of a virtual stranger: 'I've never spoken to her but she's got a mean-looking face'. 'I can't say I like him, he's got a really cold look in his eyes'.

What is self-evident for human faces, though, is not self-evident for other similar-looking creatures such as squirrels, or swans. Faced with a flock of swans, we would see them alright but we would not expect to be able to tell them apart – though they are different, just as individual faces are different. It is possible to learn to distinguish between them.

P. P. G. Bateson reports a striking instance of a graduate student, Dafila Scott, who had come to know a flock of Bewick swans so well that she claimed she could identify around 450 of them individually. She had given them all names. To test her claim Bateson photographed more than a hundred of the swans and asked her to name them – which she did. At a later date he then tested her again with a sample of the photographs and found her success in naming the swans almost perfect. 'She expressed surprise,' Bateson reports, 'that anyone should have doubted her ability since most people can recognise a large number of human faces' (Bateson, 1977: 247).

Though Dafila Scott distinguished the Bewick swans, she did not necessarily know how she did it any more than the rest of us know what it is that enables us to recognise and discriminate faces. It was not through language. Certainly she gave each swan a name, but the names were no more than tags or labels that allowed her to refer to the individual swans once she had distinguished them. It was not the names that allowed her to tell the swans apart.

People have names too, of course, but it is not their names that allow us to recognise them and tell them apart. If I have a friend you do not know and I tell you her name, Alice Maxwell, I have not translated my familiarity with my friend into words. I have simply given you the tag you might use once you identify her for yourself.

If I want to go further and translate something of my familiarity with Alice into words, then I will have to use some means other than her name. Suppose I want you to know what she looks like – visual awareness that I have but you do not – how far will language enable me to succeed, such that you will come to have, from my words, some familiarity with her face?

To get a toe-hold on the problem, try it for yourself with the face of someone you know well. How will you set about it? Could you describe your chosen face in such a way that your speaker-meaning would converge at all closely with the meaning a hearer could construct from your words?

If it seems difficult, this should not be surprising. Experimental studies of the role played by words in face recognition suggest that we remember and recognise people largely independently of language. Goldstein and Chance carried out a set of experiments which:

> contrasted face recognition performance of subjects asked to respond verbally – either to describe or associate to the faces – with that of subjects who were instructed merely to look-to-remember and other subjects who judged the faces for age and did not anticipate a later memory test.
>
> Goldstein and Chance, 1981:101

One week later the various groups differed little in recognition performance.

Furthermore

> those subjects who had made verbal responses to the faces viewed earlier were also asked to recall their verbalizations as well as to recognise the faces. To a striking degree subjects were unable – even fairly generally and when simultaneously they were positive that they recognised a face – to recall what they had said about the faces a week earlier. Or looked at another way, the faces very infrequently called up the same verbal responses on second presentation.

'It is difficult,' the researchers concluded, 'to see how such non-retrievable verbal descriptions aided recognition' (Goldstein and Chance, 1981: 101).

One major difficulty any of us would come up against in trying to characterise a face in words was summed up by art historian, E.

Gombrich, when he observed that: 'We have not one face but a thousand different faces' (Gombrich, 1972: 3). Faces are constantly in movement, always changing. What we recognise as the 'same' face is in fact a host of slightly different faces.

This enormous plasticity owes a great deal to the fact that human beings have more separate muscles in their faces than any other animal. Perhaps this partly explains why the famous mne-monist 'S' studied by Luria could not easily remember faces. He complained that they were too mobile, too changeable for him to construct a clear image.

Setting the problem of mobility aside, however, how will you set about trying to translate your familiarity with your chosen face into words? Will you, for instance, try first to characterise the face as a whole, or will you list individual features? If you begin with the whole, will you choose shape: round, thin, fat, oval, square . . . ; or attractiveness: plain, striking, beautiful, delicate, coarse . . . ; or characteristic facial expression: timid, kindly, miserable, lively . . . ?

There is no doubt that the English language makes available a rich pool of words and expressions to draw from. The limits of language do not stem from any poverty in words. The problem lies rather in finding a satisfactory match between what we 'know' through the senses and what we can say.

Your chosen face may appear to you 'round' and 'sweet' and 'kindly', for instance. This may seem a perfectly adequate charac-terisation for you as speaker, but then you already have the particular face in mind. You are selecting from your sense of a familiar face a few salient characteristics. A hearer interpreting your words does so from an entirely different vantage point. He has no face in mind, he has to start from scratch – how could he possibly converge on the face you know so well from such a broad description?

An obvious way of filling out your characterisation is to list individual features – shape and colour of eyes, set of mouth, type of hair and so on. But which features should you choose? Are some more significant than others?

An opinion poll once asked respondents which features of the face and head drew their glance and held their attention. Three out of five of this particular sample chose eyes: hair came next, chosen by just under a quarter (Jones, 1977). More rigorous experimental techniques have been used by psychologists of perception to try

and discover what features we particularly attend to in recognising faces. Results, not surprisingly, vary, but there is some
evidence that upper face features, in particular, hair, attract more
attention than lower ones, at least among Caucasians; also that the
right side of the face is seen as more representative of the
appearance of a person than the left.

In summing up the results of recent research, Shepherd, Davies
and Ellis nevertheless urge a measure of caution, particularly in
attributing too much importance to hair:

> Generally, we look at the faces of others to pick up signals
> relevant for social intercourse . . . For such purposes, the hair is
> a cue of no value, and the eyes are by far the most important
> feature . . . We also use the face as a source of information about
> the emotional state or mood of a person, and the parts of the face
> yielding this information are the brows, eyes and
> mouth . . . Different parts of the face are attended to according
> to the task confronting the individual, and generalization from
> one kind of task, say recognition memory, to another task, say
> emotional labelling, cannot be made.
>
> > Shepherd, Davies, Ellis, 1981: 130–1

Suppose instead of selecting a few features, you tried to list all
the features of your chosen face as fully and as faithfully as you
could: hair, forehead, eyes, eyebrows, cheeks, nose, mouth, ears,
chin, neck. Try it. Describe each feature: 'Short, wavy, greyish hair
with a slight fringe . . . ' 'Lined forehead . . . ' 'Wide blue-grey
eyes . . . ' and so on. Give as much detail as you wish – though
you may find even recalling each individual feature difficult:
'Many of us would be unable to describe the individual features of
our closest friends,' Gombrich notes, 'the colour of their eyes, the
exact shape of their noses, but this uncertainty does not impair our
feeling of familiarity with their features which we would pick out
among a thousand because we respond to their characteristic
expression' (Gombrich, 1972: 8).

Suppose you did succeed in drawing up such a list, how far does
this solve the problem? Will this detailed list of parts add up to a
whole identifiable face for your hearer?

To find out you would have to try it for yourself with a
co-operative partner. We would predict, though, that your hearer
would find it difficult to arrive at an image of a distinct individual

from your list. All you can reasonably hope to achieve is to give him some idea of what your chosen face does *not* look like which can be useful for picking someone out from a crowd.

But why should such a description be inadequate? Why should it be so difficult to achieve convergence between a speaker-meaning for a list of facial features – carefully compiled from the speaker's memory of the familiar face – and the 'meaning', the 'face' a hearer might construct?

Much of the difficulty lies in our uncertain understanding of the relation between parts and wholes. You who know your chosen face know it as a whole. Yet the only way in which language enables you to express that whole is by breaking it down into component parts. Language is linear, words have to come out one after another, marks on a page are arranged in lines, successively. Much of our perception, on the other hand, is holistic, non-linear. Trying to describe a face in words amounts to forcing non-linear visual awareness into a linear device.

Aarsleff tells a story about Condillac's method of teaching that reminds us that the relation of parts to wholes, wholes to parts, is an old problem:

> It was one of Condillac's favourite pedagogical and epistemolo-gical devices to place his young Prince of Parma before a window with shutters that for a brief moment were opened to give him a view of the landscape. In remembering and talking about this landscape, the young man was forced to analyse the instantaneous unitary tableau he had seen into the elements he recalled as single units – trees, shrubbery, bushes, fences, gro-ves, and the like. He was forced to think sequentially because discourse is linear.
>
> Aarsleff, 1982: 30

Condillac saw it as a strength of language that it forced his young pupil to analyse his experience, describing what he took in globally in an ordered succession of words. We are struck not so much by what is gained, but by what is lost in the lack of congruence between the holistic nature of perception and the linear nature of language.

The relation of parts to wholes is a problem not only in face recognition but in pattern recognition more generally. How do we recognise a pattern? By putting together the parts in order to form the whole? By recognising a whole which subsequently allows us to identify the parts? In which case is the identification of the parts – reversing what we generally believe – a consequence of the recognition of the whole, not a step in the process of recognition?

Does the expression of a person's eyes, for example, depend upon the whole face in such a way that the eyes would be unrecognisable if viewed out of context, say through a narrow slit – in isolation? Is it a certain expression of the eyes that brings out a particular curve of the nose which would not be noticed if the nose were in another face? The nose too in its own context may give a certain twist to the smile which may affect the expression in the eyes.

Wittgenstein summed up this interdependence aphoristically in the *Philosophical Investigations*: 'A smiling mouth *smiles* only in a human face' (Wittgenstein, 1953: 583).

The relation between parts and wholes remains an unresolved problem dividing researchers on face recognition. In recognising a face it appears that the perception of the whole selects the features essential for recognition. Yet the whole in its turn is selected by the features.

A reciprocity that remains a mystery.

*   *   *

One of the reasons we cannot readily translate our familarity with faces into words lies, paradoxically, in what is generally seen as one of the strengths of language: the way it helps us impose some order on the 'flux of perceptions, sensations and emotions' that might otherwise be our experience of living.

Language, very broadly, is organised around similarities, around the activity of identifying and grouping objects and people, events and activities, with something in common. The word 'apple', for instance, allows us to pick out a particular set of objects with the characteristics we have learnt to associate with 'being an apple'. It allows us to talk about a specific apple, or apples in general, to ask for an apple when none are present or to speculate on whether apples may one day cease to exist.

Underlying our ordinary, everyday use of the word 'apple', however, is an assumption: the assumption that the similarities between individual apples outweigh their differences. If we did

not make this assumption, we would need a different word for
each individual apple, and a new word for each new apple since
none are absolutely identical. This would not be language as we
know it. This would be language organised around naming: such
a language would not half so readily help us impose order upon
our world.

'Face', like 'apple', is another of the types of object we mark
through language. A 'face' (in one of its senses at least) sits on top
of the human body and is made up of a number of features: eyes,
mouth, forehead, nose and so on. We can talk about 'faces' just as
we can talk about 'apples': 'A pound of apples, please.' 'We
looked out at the crowd and saw a sea of faces'.

When it comes to faces, however, the assumption we make
readily enough for apples – or squirrels, or swans – the assumption that the similarities between individuals outweigh the differences – does not hold. When it comes to faces, the differences are
far more significant than the similarities. Except in vast crowds we
do not so much see 'faces' as individual faces, different from one
another, different people, different characters: 'The face is the
index of the mind'.

A speaker who says of a stranger: 'I saw her face' cannot hope
for close convergence between his and a hearer's meaning. He has
a particular face in mind which the hearer cannot know from the
word 'face'. A speaker who says 'I have an apple' on the other
hand, can hope for much closer convergence.

When it comes to faces then, an apparent strength of language
becomes a serious limitation. 'The human face', it has been said,
'is one basic recipe in a multitude of variations' (Penry, 1971: 11).
Language provides us with a means of expressing the basic
recipe – the word 'face' – but is poor on the variations between
individual faces – which is what really matters to us.

*   *   *

Intuitively we are aware of the limitations of language for passing
on to others what we know independently of words. We have
become adept at finding ways of getting round the problem
whenever we can.

Suppose you really do have to describe someone you know. You
cannot go to the airport to pick up your mother for instance; a

friend agrees to go in your place and wants to know what she looks like.

The most obvious way of getting round the limitations of language is to cut it out altogether. Show your friend a photograph of your mother. Let him see for himself. The very worst photograph will serve him better than your most carefully-chosen words.

If you do have a photograph then language can play a very useful ancillary role, helping him modify what he sees: 'Her hair is much shorter now', for instance, or 'She's lost a lot of weight since that was taken'. The likelihood of some degree of convergence between your speaker-meaning and his hearer-meaning is infinitely greater now that you are not relying on words alone.

If you do not have a photograph to hand you can suggest your friend uses your mother's name as a means of getting her to identify herself. Either via the PA system or by holding up a card with her name written boldly enough for her to see.

If she is short-sighted, or the PA system notorious for being incomprehensible, then you are thrown back on language, though not necessarily on direct description. All your friend has to do is to pick your mother out from the crowd coming off the plane. A single salient characteristic *might* be sufficient to enable him to do this. If your mother has blue hair, for instance, or is in the Salvation Army and arriving in uniform, this information may well be enough to rule out all the other people on the flight.

Not everyone has salient, unmistakable characteristics, however. If your mother is one who does not, then you can try another way of getting round the problem: using language not to try and convert into words your own experience but rather to tap your friend's own. Using language to tap relevant experience is often an effective way of circumventing the limits of straight description.

Instead of describing her directly try comparing her to someone your friend is already familiar with. Does she look, even remotely, like someone in the public eye, for instance? 'She looks a bit like the Queen', you might say – or Joan Collins, in the unlikely event that she does. Provided your friend is familiar with her lookalike, you will have come closer to convergence with these few words than if you had tried any amount of direct description.

What these various strategies show is that much of the time in using language we are offering clues to one another as to what we mean. Some clues are pretty straightforward. We solve them straightaway. Others are more cryptic. In this respect language is more like a crossword puzzle than a description: from the clues a speaker gives, a hearer has to construct a meaning he hopes corresponds to what the speaker has in mind.

There remains the possibility, of course, that your mother really does not look like anyone else, and if you do not have a photograph, and she is too short-sighted to see a card with her name on it, then you appear to be stuck within the limitations of language.

Yet even then, even if she does not look like anyone else, has no salient characteristics, it is still possible to try working with, not against, the grain of language, to remain conscious of the need to try and tap your friend's own experience. Look around you. Is there someone you can both see who shares some characteristic with your mother? If so, point her out: 'She looks a bit like that woman at the till'. And if you are reduced to listing features, you still do not need to rely entirely on words: instead of simply saying, for instance, that she has 'short, grey, wavy hair' – see if there is anyone around who has hair like hers. Or use mutual acquaintances: 'Her hair is about Jane's length' or 'It's a similar style to Rachel's hair'. The colour – not just grey but – pointing – something like that shade, perhaps darker – her colouring is a bit like mine . . . the possibilities are endless.

Bear in mind what problem your listener is facing. Accept that language is inadequate to describe directly. So do not rely on it. As a speaker, look at your words as though you were a hearer. That way your friend is going to stand some chance at least of finding your mother at the airport!

14
When a Face Really Matters

Ordinarily we see faces, recognise faces, recall faces privately, for ourselves. We are not often required to try to translate these skills into words.

Occasionally though it comes to matter whether we can say what we saw. When a crime is committed, for instance, the police question victims and witnesses. If you were the victim of a mugging, detectives will press you for a description of your attacker. If you were a witness who was walking by and saw the mugger running off, the police will want you to tell them what manner of man you saw.

More serious this, and more difficult, than your mother at the airport. You saw a stranger, perhaps only fleetingly. How well do you remember him? And if you can recall him, how well can you transfer your recall to the police?

The police have long been aware of the limitations of language to provide them with adequate descriptions of unknown suspects. Graham Davies reports that the great French forensic scientist, Alphonse Bertillon, became increasingly exasperated at the short-comings of verbal descriptions when, as a young man in the 1880s, he worked in the office of the Prefecture de Police. In an attempt to get round the limitations of language, he began to develop a totally different, visual, approach to identification, beginning by cutting out isolated facial features from photographs of criminals in the police archives, and arranging them systematically by size and shape.

Once classified and labelled, the photographs of features formed the basis for the first face-recall system: *portrait parlé*, originally used to help detectives retain information about a criminal whose identity and appearance was known. Forerunner of modern face-recall systems such as Identikit and Photofit, *portrait parlé* also came to be used as an aid for witnesses to describe the appearance of unknown suspects (Davies, 1981: 227).

Face-recall systems which use a directly visual technique are what police use to circumvent the limitations of language, at least in serious cases. Identikit and Photofit are the best-known, Identikit being one of the first modern systems, a version of which is still used, especially in the United States. Photofit replaced Identikit in Britain some years ago and is used in many countries throughout the world.

Like all face recall systems, Identikit and Photofit break the face down into component features which witnesses are then helped to build up into a composite. In the original Identikit system (now largely superseded by a photographic version) the features were in the form of line drawings printed on transparent acetate sheets. The composite face could then be built up by superimposing the sheets. The main features included in the kit were: hairlines, eyes (over 100 variations each); chins, lips, noses (40–50 variations each). Eyebrows, beards, scars, glasses etc could be added in by overlays, while further detail could be drawn in by hand using a chinagraph pencil.

Photofit is based on a system of facial topography devised by its inventor, Jacques Penry, and uses photographs of features printed on thin card. The composite face is assembled by selecting features and fitting them into a special frame which can be adjusted to take account of the shape of the face. A basic white male kit could include hairline and ears (about 200 variations); eyes and eyebrows (around 100 variations); nose, cheeks (70–80 variations each). Additional kits allow female, Afro-Asian and Arab faces to be built up while extra detail can be drawn in by hand on the transparent cover of the frame.

Face-recall systems such as Identikit and Photofit are designed to be used by witnesses helped by experienced operators. In principle at least verbal language can be kept strictly to a minimum, since the task of the witness is not to describe in words the eyes or hair or mouth of the suspect, but to select from a large set of possible eyes and hairlines and mouths the one closest to what they remember of the person they saw.

In serious assault cases this can be done, though not easily, from a hospital bed by a victim still in intensive care who can indicate by slight movements whether the feature offered by the operator is close or quite different to the assailant's. On rare occasions too, when no interpreter was available, Photofit composites have been assembled in England by witnesses unable to speak any English at all.

In cases where language is barely used, however, the results are not necessarily good. Experienced Photofit operators prefer to be able to use language – not to elicit descriptions but to comfort victims or witnesses or to get them into the right frame of mind for the task of building up the picture.

Victims of crime are often shocked and upset and may need to give vent to their feelings perhaps with a torrent of words. A good detective will have learnt to listen patiently, knowing that the usefulness of the eventual result will depend in large part on the state of the victim when he or she gave it.

Even with witnesses not so directly involved, there may still be a need to get them to relax or to establish a rapport through apparently trivial uses of language to talk about the garden or the weather or the dog.

The operator will generally start with words, asking basic questions to establish the assailant's race, age, build. He may ask too whether there were any particularly salient characteristics. A victim might recall for instance, that the attacker had a red face or particularly bloodshot eyes, neither of which would show up well in the Photofit, but can be added in words. This is very different to simply being told that an unknown man had 'bloodshot eyes' – for there would be no very clear eyes to impose a notion of 'bloodshot' on. Once a Photofit picture gives some idea of the eyes, then the verbal description 'bloodshot' is immediately more informative.

There are no set procedures for compiling Photofit pictures, but they are normally built up by trying first to establish basic facial shape. Usually the operator will start by offering one by one the set of possible hairline and ears, letting the witness go through as slowly as they like without interfering or making suggestions. Once one is selected and inserted into the special frame, the next stage would normally be to add the chin – chins look odd on their own, but if the hairline and ears are already in place, adding the chin allows the facial shape to start emerging. When the shape of the face is established eyes and other features are added in.

Face-recall systems largely bypass words, tapping a witness's visual memory direct. This does not mean, however, that talk is discouraged during a Photofit session which can take several hours. Witnesses will often try to express, for instance, why a particular picture seems wrong – for even if they do not remember well enough to arrive at a good likeness they may still have a strong sense that the likeness being constructed is poor.

Some verbal descriptions can nonplus though: 'He had a common, working-class sort of a face', one detective was told by a woman witness. Certainly people do talk in terms of facial stereotypes: 'He looks a typical Scot/bureaucrat/barman . . . '. Haydn Ellis and Jean Shepherd tried testing people's stereotypes to see if they had any basis in fact. They found little consistency, however, with individuals giving labels as widely-different as 'stately-home-owner' and 'manual worker' to the same face.

In some cases subjects may be sidetracked into seeking a particular facial expression – 'It isn't evil enough', they may say of the Photofit face. 'He had a really nasty face' or 'The eyes were much more piercing'. Not unnaturally assault victims in particular can have difficulty sometimes in separating the man committing the crime from the same man in a more neutral setting. A detective who is good at his job will not try and deny their experience or convert it into the kind of description he could better use. Instead he will accept it, then try and get them to shift their perspective: 'Yes, but now can you try and imagine what he'll look like when I go round to see him.'

In cases such as assault or rape, building up the Photofit picture can occasionally have quite a dramatic effect unleashing sobs or even hysteria. In such cases Photofits are sometimes built up quickly and decisively, though experimental evidence has not shown that such victims are more accurate in their recall than people involved in less emotive incidents.

In all cases detectives need to assess how reliable their witnesses are. Some remember little but are only too anxious to please. One detective recalled an occasion when he went to see an elderly woman to get a Photofit description from her and inadvertently left open the resulting picture from his last visit which had been concerned with a completely different case. The old woman spotted it: 'Yes, that's him', she said with great confidence.

Face-recall systems such as Photofit certainly help police get around the limitations of language by allowing visual descriptions to emerge without the mediation of words. Computer-based systems are being developed which could greatly improve the quality of the likeness a witness can achieve.

Though such systems undoubtedly have great advantages over verbal descriptions, they do, however, have their own shortcomings. They are time-consuming and expensive, and therefore reserved for more serious cases. Many forces do not have experienced operators, which can considerably reduce their effectiveness. Perhaps more serious: they are based on the simplifying assumption that people remember faces in terms of constituent features in spite of evidence that recall and recognition also involve more global processing.

Despite these shortcomings though, when a face really matters, it is undoubtedly more effective to show than to say what you saw. Particularly so, considering that the aim of compiling a Photofit likeness is not so much to arrive at a picture of a specific individual but at a type. Face-recall systems are at their best in helping narrow down the range of possible suspects – there even the roughest likeness can be good enough to eliminate the others.

15
Educating the Senses

Just as most of our ordinary recognition and recall of faces takes place independently of language, so too does much of the rest of our sensory experience. Most of the time we touch and taste and smell without reflection. We just do it, privately and individually, without trying to translate our experience into words.

If we want to compare what we see or hear or taste with other people, however, then we do need language, even if it is inadequate. How otherwise are we to know how others are responding to music or to our new colour scheme or to a wine none of us has tasted before?

We need language too when we want to improve the performance of our senses, to learn to make more, and more subtle, discriminations. For anyone seriously interested in wine-tasting or perfumes or plane-spotting, tasting, or sniffing or staring up at passing aircraft unsystematically is not enough. We have to learn to organise what we experience through our senses, remember it, compare the taste of one wine, for instance, with another, a fine wine with a mediocre one, an acidic wine with a mellow. We have to devise means of recognising the same types of wines or planes or perfumes when we come across them again. We have to educate our senses.

Language is not essential to the process of educating our senses. The student who learnt to discriminate among the 450 Bewick swans, for example, did not do so through language – though she did use names to label the discriminations once she had made them.

If she had wanted to exchange views with another expert on the subtle differences between the swans, however, then she would have needed recourse to words. Experts have usually developed 'technical terms' – what outsiders sometimes call 'jargon' – for discussing among themselves what they know so much more about than other people. When we learn a new skill we generally do so with the help of experts, in person, or through books. Part of what we learn is their 'jargon', their way of talking: about the wines we are learning to distinguish, for instance, or the planes we can now identify.

One difficulty experts can discover in trying to pass on some of their skill to novices is just how much there is that they know but cannot put into words. Master of Wine, Michael Broadbent, lists grape varieties for the benefit of beginners in his *Pocket Guide to Wine Tasting*. On the Gamay grape he writes: 'Its most marked characteristics are a charmingly forthcoming and fruity bouquet, unique in character – difficult to describe but fairly easy to recognise' (Broadbent, 1982: 35).

'Difficult to describe, but fairly easy to recognise'. Just as Dafila Scott recognised, but probably could not have described, many of the more subtle differences she saw between the Bewick swans.

If even the experts can have problems in translating subtle sense discriminations into words, this can have serious consequences for teaching and learning. It is not easy to teach what you know but do not really know how you know.

Even where the expert, the teacher, is able to translate some of his skill into words, it does not follow that the novice, lacking experience and expertise, will converge at all closely on the expert's words. If the words used to teach stand for 'terrain' accessible only with skill and experience, how can the novice hope more than vaguely to understand?

Michael Polanyi, radiologist-turned-philosopher, gives a vivid account from his own experience as a medical student of the difficult task the novice faces, confronted by the experts' language, expected to understand and learn before he has acquired the skills and experience that would make the words fall into place. In *Personal Knowledge*, he writes:

> Think of a medical student attending a course in the X-ray diagnosis of pulmonary diseases. He watches in a darkened room shadowy traces on a fluorescent screen placed against a patient's chest, and hears the radiologist commenting to his assistants in technical language, on the significant features of these shadows.

> At first the student is completely puzzled. For he can see in the X-ray picture of a chest only the shadows of the heart and the

ribs, with a few spidery blotches between them. The experts seem to be romancing about figments of their imagination; he can see nothing that they are talking about.

With time, however, the student gains experience:

as he goes on listening for a few weeks, looking carefully at ever new pictures of different cases, a tentative understanding will dawn on him; he will gradually forget about the ribs and begin to see the lungs. And eventually, if he perseveres intelligently, a rich panorama of significant details will be revealed to him: of physiological variations and pathological changes, of scars, of chronic infections and signs of acute disease.

From seeing little and understanding even less:

He has entered a new world. He still sees only a fraction of what the experts can see, but the pictures are definitely making sense now and *so do most of the comments made on them* [*our italics*]. He is about to grasp what he is being taught; it has clicked. Thus, at the very moment when he has learned the language of pulmonary radiology, the student will also have learned to understand pulmonary radiograms.

Polanyi concludes:

The two can only happen together. Both halves of the problem set to us by an unintelligible text, referring to an unintelligible substance, jointly guide our efforts to solve them, and they are solved eventually together by discovering a conception which comprises a joint understanding of both the words and the things.

Polanyi, 1964: 101

Polanyi's account of learning to understand the language used by experts in interpreting X-rays offers a glimpse of that exhilarating moment in learning when language and sense experience suddenly click – when words and experience snap together. Not only was the student now learning to see what previously had been invisible, he was simultaneously able to express something of what he saw.

Before the click takes place, medical students have to undergo a lengthy training in clinical medicine, struggling, even if they are not explicitly aware of it, against the limitations of language for expressing sensory experience.

At the heart of the problem lies the inevitable gap between what the expert, in this case the consultant physician or surgeon, has learnt, in part through his senses, about the signs and symptoms of disease and the little the medical student, with his limited experience, knows.

As we saw earlier with the Bewick swans or the bouquet of the Gamay grape, one difficulty in using language to bridge the gap between an expert's sensory knowledge and a novice's sensory ignorance is that the expert's skills can only partially be distilled into words.

Some clues a physician responds to while examining a patient, he may be aware of only tacitly – even though it may be the clues on the fringes of his awareness that prove crucial in guiding him to a diagnosis.

The skilled clinician may be something of an artist, using his senses in ways that have become largely intuitive to penetrate a patient's condition. Inevitably the language he uses to express that special knowledge, gained through long experience of educating the senses, will offer a crude approximation to the richness of the knowledge itself.

In the case of the Bewick swans or the Gamay grape, the consequences of the expert's inability to say all he knows are none too serious. When it comes to medicine, however, the need to overcome problems in passing on skills is more acute.

Essentially the budding clinician, being unable to draw directly on the consultant's experience, has to be helped to acquire the necessary expertise for himself. He has to educate his senses – sight, hearing, smell, touch, feeling – so that when he examines a patient he can see or feel for himself what is normal, what is not normal, interpret the signs and symptoms of disease.

Part of the way he learns to diagnose is by watching the experts in action, listening to their language, responding to their questions. Typically groups of students accompany experienced doctors as they do their 'rounds' in the wards of the teaching hospital. During these sessions the students observe patients, examine patients, listen to their hearts, feel their lumps and swellings, under the consultant's instruction. The idea is that gradually they will gain the visual, aural, tactile skills that now seem natural to the consultant, though there was a time when he was just as ignorant as his students.

Students may be called upon to 'notice', for instance, the complexion of a patient: to an expert the colour of a patient's skin can be a useful diagnostic.

Colour terms are notoriously difficult; finding words to characterise the colour of a patient's complexion is a particularly tricky problem for the apprentice physician who has as yet little experience of the relation of complexion to disease. He can see the patient perfectly well, just as Polanyi could see the 'shadowy traces' on the screen in the darkened room, but he does not know what he should be noticing.

In his book *The Clinical Experience*, Paul Atkinson reports as by no means exceptional an incident that illustrates the medical students' difficulties:

> Dr Cartwright got one of the students to examine the patient's cardio-vascular system . . .
> Meanwhile the doctor asked James Bury to come round and look at the patient.
> Bury said he thought the patient's face and neck looked 'rather red'.
> Dr Cartwright queried this, and Bury changed his answer to 'yellow'.
> Dr Cartwright called over another of the students and asked for his opinion on the patient's colouring. He replied he would say the patient was 'well-tanned'.
> Dr Cartwright agreed, and wrote 'well-tanned' on the blackboard.
>
> Atkinson, 1981: 98

Though the patient presumably remained the same colour throughout, within a few moments the words used for his complexion changed from 'rather red' to 'yellow' to 'well-tanned'. When Bury's original 'rather red' was challenged, he changed his description to 'yellow', not because the patient now looked different, but because the expert, his teacher, Dr Cartwright, did not accept 'rather red' as an appropriate description. As it turned out, Dr Cartwright did not accept 'yellow' either so in the end it was left to another student to provide the 'well-tanned' he was prepared to allow.

What the students were doing here was trying to learn to see as an expert would see, at the same time as learning to match what they saw with words – words an expert, or at least this particular expert, would accept. The expert, Dr Cartwright, for his part, was using the students' words 'rather red', 'yellow', 'well-tanned' as a way of assessing whether they were seeing as they should. His problem was that he could not know from what they said publicly what they were seeing privately. The whole process is a rough and ready one that relies on students slowly and gradually coming to understand their experience better and adjusting their language to reflect their growing expertise.

The apparently more concrete sense of touch, 'palpating' in medical terminology, can be just as difficult to learn to translate into appropriate words. During one session a consultant surgeon was demonstrating a swelling in a female patient's neck. Atkinson reports his efforts to get the students to feel what he felt:

> So here is this swelling in her neck, and there is no doubt about the state of this – no doubt about her thyroid state.
> The consultant got one of the girl students to come and examine the thyroid.
> She did so and reported her findings to us, 'There is a soft swelling – with soft edges – not nodules'.
> The surgeon replied, 'I thought it was nodular myself'.

Here the expert uses language to try and direct the student's palpating, alerting her to the possibility of a different interpretation of what she feels. He fails.

> 'I couldn't find any nodules.' She palpated the patient's neck once more. 'No, I can't find any nodules' (hesitantly).
> 'You're hedging. Let's get another opinion'. The surgeon asked a second student to come and examine the patient.
> 'It feels quite smooth in the right lobe, but in the isthmus there might be a discrete lump. But otherwise I agree.'
> The surgeon made no immediate comment, but when the patient had gone back to her bed in the ward he said that we would see who was right tomorrow, when he operated on the

patient. He told the students to be sure to see a specimen of the patient's gland.

Atkinson, 1981: 99

The expert had tried, via the term 'nodular', to direct the students' examination, to teach them to feel as he felt, as a trained surgeon felt. When their words suggested they did not feel as he did, he did not say they were wrong, though in the event, after the operation had been carried out his description – nodular – turned out to be the most appropriate.

It should have been an easier task to agree on what was felt than to agree on the colour of a complexion. In this case the consultant and the students were 'palpating' the same physical object in the outer world. Either the thyroid was nodular or it was not.

The students were facing a more complex problem, however, than that of simply finding the appropriate words. In the case of the first girl student, what she felt did not correspond to what she understood as 'nodular' even though the tissue when examined turned out to be what a surgeon would call 'nodular'. What we do not know is whether the adjustment she would have to make was in her use of language: she had felt all the expert had felt but would not up to then have termed that 'nodular'. Or whether she could not feel the nodules, and would have to refine her palpation technique.

Not all consultants are even sympathetic to the novice's plight. If students observe but do not have the necessary experience to know what they should expect to see, this surely puts some onus on the expert to give at least a little guidance. Atkinson reports elsewhere the following incident that occurred during a consultant's rounds.

Flanked by a cluster of students in their first year of clinical studies, the consultant stopped at the foot of a patient's bed. 'What do you observe about this patient?' he asked one of the students without preamble, giving no hint at all of what he had in mind. The unfortunate student had no idea what he was supposed to observe:

'He's got grey hair,' he ventured. This was in fact quite true – the patient was a youngish man with a full head of grey hair. 'So have I,' replied the consultant drily, raising a laugh from the others. 'No – I meant he was a young man with grey hair,' the student tried to recover but to no avail.

Atkinson, 1978: 83–91

The 'correct' answer, it turned out, was that the patient was in a lot of pain. That was what the 'teacher' had in mind, expecting his students to be mind-readers – as teachers often do.

Some less arrogant consultants still get frustrated when their students do not seem to hear or see or feel as they should. Atkinson describes the experience of a group of students learning to hear through the stethoscope the distinctive pattern of heart sounds characteristic of a number of different conditions – mitral stenosis, aortic stenosis and so forth:

In the course of bedside teaching, the consultant told the students that he wanted them all to listen to the patient's chest and then come away from the bedside and tell him what they had found . . . Adrian was the first to listen to the patient's chest, and having done so he went off to report to the consultant. . . . When Adrian came back he reported to John Finch, who asked him what he had found. But Adrian said he was 'sworn to secrecy', . . . He did vouchsafe, however, that he had been given a 'bollocking' by the consultant. One by one the students completed their brief examinations, bending silently over [the patient], and listening intently through their stethoscopes [the patient himself said and did nothing]. One by one they left – reluctantly it appeared – and went to explain their findings to the consultant. One by one they came back to the group by the patient's bed, mostly with rather shamefaced expressions. As they did so, and began to compare notes, it became clear that whatever the 'classic' manifestations, the students' hearing was by no means consistent with what their teacher had expected. John Finch whispered to us that he had been called a 'moron'; David Dean . . . 'a buffoon'. They seemed to be rather amused by the dressing down that they had all received. It emerged that a couple of them had correctly identified *some* of the patient's distinctive signs, *none* of them had produced a correct description of the overall pattern of heart sounds. When they had all finished, the consultant physician returned, and had them all have another listen to the patient's chest, to try and hear what they had been supposed to hear in the first place.

Atkinson, 1981: 96–7

'To try and hear what they had been supposed to hear in the first place.' In this expression Atkinson captures the student clinician's fundamental problem. Before finding the right words, he has to learn to have the right experience. The consultant physician cannot have the experience for him – the experience ultimately is private. He can, of course, castigate them when they are wrong – 'buffoon', 'moron' – give them a round 'bollocking', encourage them when they seem to be 'getting warmer'. But there is no way of ensuring by rule that the student will get it right, hear what the experience of the consultant is guiding him to hear, feel what the fingers of the physician feel. In the end all the physician can do is urge them to 'Hear it this way', 'Feel it nodular'.

Achieving convergence in the use of medical language involves a long, slow apprenticeship to a good teacher with no guarantee of success at the end.

The student needs receptive qualities as much as the consultant needs his experience. Then, by a kind of osmosis, a degree of convergence through the means of language, may be achieved, some understanding may take place.

The physician's skill, like any connoisseurship, is transmitted in large part by example rather than by prescription, command or rule. The medical student is almost imperceptibly acquiring an art of doing as much as a body of knowledge from his textbooks.

The language expressing that art is also learned by doing as much as listening or reading. And the doing – the use of sight, hearing, touch and feeling – is only with considerable difficulty converted into a common language the experts can use and understand.

The role of language in this learning process is adjectival to the richness of the experience the educated senses afford. And convergence among the experts is only easier, never easy.

16

Talking about Tasting: the language of wine

'I was convinced forty years ago – and the conviction remains to this day – that in wine tasting and wine talk, there is an enormous amount of humbug.'

T. G. Shaw, *Wine, The Vine and The Cellar*, 1863

Much of our everyday talk about food and drink is actually about likes and dislikes, sometimes as a kind of running commentary to a meal: 'Don't think much of this wine, do you? Tastes like vinegar'. 'How's your steak? Very nice. Yes, very nice and tender'. If we are guests politeness may make our 'commentary' somewhat less than frank.

Likes and dislikes aside, we rarely try to translate into words the sensations we experience when eating and drinking, perhaps because we know how difficult it would be. If someone wants to know what caviar or kumquats taste like, better they taste some for themselves.

The closest we normally come is to pick out a salient characteristic: 'I can't drink this liqueur. It's far too sweet'. 'Be careful, the curry's very hot'. 'Was the soup alright? Mm, a bit bland, I'd say'. Not that 'sweet' characterises the taste of one particular liqueur any more than 'hot' marks the taste of one specific curry. Many distinct liqueurs may be 'sweet' and many different curries 'hot'.

When we do try to translate taste into words we commonly use only the grossest categories, often involving the so-called primary tastes: sweetness (associated with the tip of the tongue), sourness (affecting the upper edges of the tongue), bitterness (back of the tongue) and saltiness (affecting the sides). Broad categories may be perfectly adequate for our purposes: if the 'sweetness' of the liqueur outweighs anything else in its taste, then 'sweet' should serve us well enough. If 'hotness' is what dominates the curry, what would be the point of trying to refine our description of its flavour?

If we want to get closer we can try, as we do for faces, to get round the limitations of language, compare the taste we are talking about with one our hearer already knows: 'What do nectarines taste like?' 'Like peaches'.

Often though the comparisons we make are simply judgements in another guise – 'These biscuits taste like damp cardboard' – intended as a joke sometimes: we order a bottle of the cheapest housewine. 'Well, what's it like?' 'Anti-freeze with just a hint of brake fluid'.

Most talk about wine is not so flippant. On the contrary, wine is big business with millions of gallons produced and marketed every year. The language of wine, more than the language for other tastes, has been developed and cultivated, spawning books and journals, TV programmes and regular columns in newspapers and magazines. Wine writing has even become a profession.

To the outsider, however, talk about wine can seem arcane. 'They seem to be romancing about figments of their imagination,' Polanyi wrote, describing the student radiologist's bafflement at what the experts were reporting they found in the X-ray pictures. 'Romancing about figments of their imagination' can seem to the ordinary drinker what wine buffs are doing too. 'It's a naïve domestic Burgundy, without any breeding, but I think you will be amused at its presumption'. So Thurber satirised them in one of his best-known cartoons.

But are wine experts fakes? Is there 'an enormous amount of humbug' in wine-tasting and wine talk? Is the whole business of expressing subtle judgements on wines and fine discriminations between wines little more than verbal display, an elaborate social game, tedious and largely meaningless to those who do not play?

These questions are worth asking if only because the problems posed by translating the impact of wines into words bring into much clearer focus the more general problem of finding an adequate language to express what we experience through our senses.

What is not always appreciated, however, is that the experts generally reserve their books and journals and regular columns for talking about only a tiny proportion of the wine that is actually produced. Most of the wine on the mass-market, while acceptable enough to drink, is a blend of different wines which inevitably in the blending lose much of their individuality. 'Ordinary wine is for talking over, not talking about', Michael Broadbent aptly summed it up (Broadbent, 1982: 8). Some of the outsider's suspicion could well be the result of pretentious amateurs claiming to discern fine qualities in unpretentious wines.

In fact most wine-tasting and talking is carried on among professionals rather than the affected amateurs who were the target of Thurber's wit. Producers, for instance, taste at various stages to assess the progress of their wines. Merchants, buying for bottling, taste. Wholesalers and institutional buyers taste at trade tastings. All these are experts who have learnt through years of experience how to judge and discriminate wines for their particular purposes. For most of them language will have played a role in their learning to discriminate. Not directly – discriminations of taste do not depend on words, but rather in helping to recall the varied impact of the many different wines they have encountered.

The difference between the expert and the novice wine-taster is similar to the difference between the medical student and the experienced clinician. The expert's senses are educated in a way the novice's are not.

Educating the senses requires educating the memory to recall sensations. You need to be able to remember different tastes so as to recognise them when you come across them again or to distinguish them from others that are similar but distinct. Words can help by acting as triggers to evoke individual tastes, allowing a new one to be identified by comparison with what has been tasted before.

Educating the sense for tasting wines is not at all straightforward though, not least because wine – like all food and drink to varying degrees – affects much more than just the tastebuds. Wine makes its impact on the subtly-interrelated senses of sight and smell as well as taste. Newcomers to wine-tasting are advised to approach each wine in a regular sequence, to judge first with the eyes, then the nose and finally the mouth: appearance, bouquet, and only then, taste.

The appearance of a fine wine can of course give pleasure simply in itself. It is not necessary to be an expert to enjoy the ruby red of a young claret held against a candle or the rich gold of a mature Sauternes. The expert, however, like the radiologist, with his educated eye, will be better-equipped to interpret what he sees.

If he is tasting 'blind' the colour of the wine – both hue and depth – will give valuable clues as to the type of wine and its age. The colour towards the rim of the glass will normally be different to the colour at the deepest point of the bowl: the experienced taster will know something of how to interpret the significance of the shading. And if he already knows the type of wine and its age, then he may be able to assess whether the colour seems right, whether this particular wine is a good specimen of its type.

Many ordinary drinkers, in contrast, know little more about the colour of wines than that most are 'red' or 'white' and a few are 'rosé'. In fact, so-called 'white' wines are wines of many different hues ranging from virtually colourless to shades of pale yellow-green, straw-yellow, gold, and – fortified wines being technically 'white' – even brown. 'Red' wines, too, can vary from purplish to near-mahogany, while in some languages, Croatian, for example, the darkest of 'red' wines are not red at all but *crn*, 'black'. 'Red' and 'white' are technical terms, it turns out, with special meanings when applied to wines.

Translating the colour of different wines into words, while not straightforward, nevertheless presents fewer problems than talking about sensations of smell and taste: 'The enormous advantage that colour has . . . is that it can be so much more easily described, recorded or matched and conveyed from one person to another', Michael Broadbent notes. 'In the last resort it can be accurately reproduced' (Broadbent, 1982: 15).

To those more knowledgeable about language than about wines, this can at first seem surprising. Words for colour are generally thought of as problematic, differing across individuals such that what I call 'green' you may well call 'blue', differing, too, apparently, across cultures as speakers of diverse languages divide up the spectrum differently.

The English colour term 'brown', for instance, has no single equivalent in French – it might be translated *brun*, *marron* or even *jaune*, according to the particular shade and kind of noun it qualifies. Russian has no straightforward equivalent to 'blue' – the words *goluboj* and *sinij*, usually translated as 'light blue' and 'dark blue', refer to what are considered distinct colours, not different shades of the same colour as their translation into English might suggest.

Compared to the problems posed by the much more firmly private sensations produced by smells and tastes, however, colour can appear easy. Colour after all is 'public'. Colour is 'out there', in the world. Colours can be set side by side, compared, matched. We can, if necessary, reach explicit agreement with others on what to call this or that particular shade of red.

A novice wine-taster can learn something of the significance of hue and depth of colour by using a chart which reproduces a range of wines as they appear in the glass from bowl to rim. By looking at the chart and looking at actual wine in a glass held against the light, the newcomer can begin to educate his eyes by seeing for himself.

In this way, using a directly visual means, the limitations of language are circumvented much as the police get round them by using face-recall systems such as Photofit. Paradoxically perhaps, it is only when the novice wine-taster has begun to see for himself something of the significance of shading and hue that the words the experts use for the colour of wines begin to fall into place.

Clarity is the other significant aspect of the appearance of a wine. With a good teacher, learning to evaluate the clarity of a wine is not too difficult. Most of us can quickly see what a 'dull cloudiness' or 'haziness' in a glass looks like and match words to what we see. We can learn by looking, by being shown. If the wine is slightly sparkling when it should not be, we should be able to see the bubbles, at least when they are pointed out, so we can learn to look for ourselves next time. If there are particles floating in the wine, we will probably see them – tartaric acid crystals in white wines, for instance. These are harmless enough, though we cannot know that without being told.

The really tricky problems arise when it comes to finding words for the myriad sensations that nose and mouth, smell and taste afford. Such problems are the more important since words can be an important element in helping build up and improve our gustatory memory.

Smell and taste are more closely related than we often realise. Brillat-Savarin saw them as inseparable:

> I am not only convinced that there is no full act of tasting without the participation of the sense of smell, but I am also tempted to believe that smell and taste form a single sense, of which the mouth is the laboratory and the nose is the chimney; or, to speak more exactly, of which one serves for the tasting of actual bodies and the other for the savouring of their gases.
>
> Fisher, 1971: 39

'Nosing' a wine, evaluating its bouquet – the second of the classic stages in tasting – is particularly important, the nose being capable of conveying more subtle messages to the brain than the mouth. To the expert the 'nose' of a wine can reveal a good deal of complex information as to youthfulness or maturity and overall quality.

When it comes to expressing the characteristics of a particular bouquet, however, Broadbent comments:

> It is difficult enough to analyse and describe most common-or-garden smells; even more so the subtleties of a refined bouquet. And if it is difficult to pin down the elements of bouquet, it is almost impossible to convey them to another person.
>
> Broadbent, 1982: 27

Nor is the problem any easier when it comes to the sensations of the mouth, the taste, the flavour. Jancis Robinson writes:

> For wine tasters there is no definitive term or mark for something as simple and distinctive as the flavour of the Gamay grape, say, let alone for the nuances it's given by the various other factors that paint the 'palate picture', such as the soil the grapes were grown in, the weather that led up to the harvest and the way the wine was made and stored.
>
> Robinson, 1983: 33

While it may be difficult to pin down the bouquet or the flavour of a wine, however, this does not mean that wine-tasters are condemned to silence. On the contrary. 'Fine wine demands to be talked about', Michael Broadbent says. 'There is a wide spectrum of words, but they more or less boil down to two categories: factual and fanciful. There is, I believe, a place for both' (Broadbent, 1982: 90).

Behind Broadbent's 'factual' and 'fanciful' lies the complex mix of public and private that goes to make up talk about wines. Some sensations of smell and taste, readily recognisable with training and experience, have a specific physical cause. Wine over-exposed to air, for instance, will be attacked by ferments turning it 'vinegary' or 'acetic'. An odour reminiscent of 'geraniums' will most probably be caused by a micro-organism derived mainly from esters formed during fermentation. A wine high in tannin is likely to be 'astringent' causing a dry, mouth-puckering effect.

Such terms – 'acetic', 'geraniums', 'astringent' – reflect primarily matters of fact about the physical world. Experts using them would thus be likely to converge quite closely.

Such 'factual' terms would normally be listed in the glossaries of useful words for wine-tasters often to be found in books about wine. Many of the other words included will be broad descriptive terms – 'powerful', 'green', 'flabby', 'lively' – used to pick out the dominant attributes of particular wines. Since smell and taste are essentially private, subjective sensations even for experts these cannot be precise terms. However, with long experience of tasting and talking and coming to agree that this wine is 'meaty', that one 'aromatic', the other 'fresh', those knowledgeable about wines come to accept a common stock of terms they individually feel they understand.

Newcomers, however, would not necessarily be able to match their impressions of wines with the words the experts use. Hearing a wine called 'spicy' or 'smoky', 'firm' or 'flinty', for instance, might leave a novice at a loss as to the characteristic the term is supposed to pick out. Is what he thinks he tastes the 'smokiness' or flintiness' the experts mean? Or is it something else, a quality he has missed? Newcomers need to taste many wines, and hear the same terms applied many times before they begin to click.

Not that all wine-tasting terms are obscure. On the contrary, some can seem self-evident. A novice hearing a wine characterised as 'cloying' or 'perfumed' or 'tart' or 'sweet', for instance, might find it straightforward to match the term and the taste. The same is less likely to be so for a word such as 'inky'. Jancis Robinson used it in a *Sunday Times Magazine* article aimed at novices. She was commenting on the way that wines made from Cabernet Sauvignon grapes can be unpleasantly astringent when young. 'Together with its high acidity,' she went on, 'this can make a young Cabernet Sauvignon taste almost inky' (Robinson, 1986).

In his glossary Broadbent defines 'inky' as: 'an unpleasant, tinny, metallic taste due to the presence of tannate of iron produced by the action of tannin on iron – a nail in a cask will have this effect. Tannate of iron is the chief constituent of ink' (Broadbent, 1982: 118). Though the novice has no way of knowing this from the word 'inky' alone, the term does alert him to the possibility that young Cabernet Sauvignon wines might have an unpleasant characteristic of some kind. If later he drinks a young claret, for instance, he may take note of its taste, while if he is interested in learning he may be prompted to discuss with more experienced tasters whether there is perhaps a trace of 'inkiness'. In this way a puzzling term can slowly become less puzzling.

The way experts have evolved a common stock of terms to pick out dominant characteristics of wines illustrates the public side of wine talk. Language plays another role too for wine-tasters, however, helping them each, individually, to recall and identify and discriminate between different wines. This is the private side of wine connoisseurship, skills each taster must acquire for himself.

The role of language is to act essentially as a 'trigger': 'If I smell Tempranillo, for instance, says Jancis Robinson, 'I say "tobacco" to myself and can therefore identify it as such' (Robinson, 1983: 167).

Some of these 'trigger words' are widely-accepted: many tasters use 'blackcurrants', for example, for the characteristic scent of the Cabernet Sauvignon grape; some find 'cedarwood' more effective. 'Raspberries' is often used to evoke the Pinot Noir; some find 'boiled beetroot' works better. Jancis Robinson was lost for a word to pin down her impressions of the Hermitage grape, Syrah. Someone volunteered their 'burnt rubber'. It clicked for her and has worked ever since. 'This story is told,' she adds, 'to encourage you to persevere if you find matching words and flavours a difficult exercise. As you will have gathered, the expression can be as absurd as you like' (Robinson, 1983: 65).

Her point is reinforced by another distinctive wine writer, Pamela Vandyke Price:

The notes people make about the smells of wines can be highly individual, and if it is helpful for you to associate a certain smell with a certain wine or type of wine, there is no need to work out some polite phrase if your meaning is adequately expressed even by something crude.

She gives the Traminer grape as an example:

If the Traminer grape smell reminds a taster of newly-ironed laundry this is a perfectly delightful and vivid description. The Traminer, to me, smells like a haystack but I have known it remind people, pleasantly and satisfactorily, of a midden.

Vandyke Price, 1976: 40

This is what Broadbent called the 'fanciful' side of wine talk. For the novice it means developing your own trigger expressions, a kind of private language that relates words with the complex array of similar but different smells and tastes fine wines provide. The aim is not to achieve correct expressions, measured against some public standard, but effective ones. Your trigger words have to work for you, helping you both to recognise and identify wines, if necessary, blind.

Words which work for you may of course work for other people too. The language is not entirely private. Novices may well start by learning some of the trigger words others use and trying to match them with what they smell and taste, only gradually gaining the confidence to develop their own.

In her glossary in *Masterglass* Jancis Robinson includes both trigger words that are widely used and some that are more personal: 'pencil shavings', for instance: 'the smell (of the wood not the lead) that I find in Cabernet Franc' or 'gummy': 'the richness that very ripe Chenin Blanc grapes can bring to a wine'.

The following short list of words from Pamela Vandyke Price's glossary in *The Taste of Wine* gives some idea of her inventiveness: assertive, crunchy, dirty, forthcoming, pinched ('mean in character'), pretty, reserved, sensitive, sick, sloppy, soggy, turned in ('withdrawn, needing a little aeration'), uncoordinated, vivacious, wet.

'Choosing words to describe wine,' Jancis Robinson says, 'is largely a matter of making comparisons with things that are not wine' (Robinson, 1983: 33). 'Goaty', 'cat's pee', 'weedy', 'gritty' and 'woofy' are all part of the language of one wine expert or another, acting as clues or triggers, helping to evoke and identify particular wines. There can be something liberating, even exhilarating, in the freedom to let the imagination run a little riot over words for wine, creating novel, personal links in the struggle to translate sense experience into language.

Broadbent comments:

One could argue that likening a bouquet to violets or saying a taste is reminiscent of truffles is not very meaningful if the listener or reader is unfamiliar with the smell of one and the flavour of the other. Yet I believe it is quite defensible to do so; analogies add extra dimensions and help other tasters identify and memorize facets.

Broadbent, 1982: 91

Pamela Vandyke Price avails herself more than most of the freedom: 'When tasting Muscadet,' she writes, 'think of the nearness of the sea to the vineyards, the west winds coming in from the Atlantic, and the variable, often wet, cold climate' (Vandyke Price, 1976: 62).

Great red wines, often Bordeaux, that have not yet reached their peak, can have a close-textured smell like 'heavy velvet curtains' (Vandyke Price, 1976: 40). An old Bordeaux may release a rather dampish smell like an unaired cellar giving it for some 'a mushroom nose.'

Personifying a wine too can sometimes help to fix its savour: some wines are obviously adolescent, not yet fully developed, another still a baby, others mature, still others past or just passing their prime. She notes too a more subtle series of distinctions that may spur the novice in his struggle to find words to fit his sensations:

> Comparisons can make the taste memory vivid by personal notes that liken a particular Pauillac to a guards officer, a St Julien to a diplomat; the mind will remember that the 1967 Bordeaux are friendly but that the 1969 rather lack charm, that the Burgundies of Firm X are slightly tarty and those of Firm Z too shy to possess wide appeal.
>
> Vandyke Price, 1976: 80

This part-private use of words to fix sensations in the memory, to make it possible to recall smells and tastes once they are gone, is a side of language that Locke did not dwell much upon.

Locke, we noted, drew two pictures. One of a man locked within his own experience of the world, a radically private man:

> Man, though he have great variety of Thoughts, and such, from which others, as well as himself, might receive Profit and Delight; yet they are all within his own Breast, invisible, and hidden from others, nor can of themselves be made appear. (III, II, 1)

Next to that picture Locke placed another, of man as a social creature, wanting, indeed needing, to break out of his isolation, create, as we suggested earlier, a 'we' side, a common world with others:

> The Comfort and Advantage of Society, not being to be had without Communication of Thoughts, it was necessary, that Man should find some external sensible Signs, whereby those invisible *Ideas*, which his thoughts are made up of, might be made known to others. (III, II, 1)

But he could have drawn a third:

> We have, in the former part of this Discourse, often, upon occasion, mentioned a *double use of Words*.
> *First*, One for the recording of our own Thoughts.
> *Secondly*, The other for the communicating of our Thoughts to others.
> As to the first of these *for the recording of our own Thoughts* for the help of our own Memories, whereby, as it were, we talk to ourselves, any Words will serve the turn. For since Sounds are voluntary and indifferent signs of any *Ideas*, a Man may use what Words he pleases, to signify his own *Ideas* to himself:and there will be no imperfection in them, if he constantly use the same sign for the same *Idea*: for then he cannot fail of having his meaning understood, wherein consists the right use and perfection of Language. (III, IX, 1–2)

This is Locke's picture of an individual using language not to communicate with others, but to help bring order into his own purely personal sensations. A language still learnt 'publicly' from others, with others, but used to make individual, private connections.

If Humpty Dumpty had restrained his own solipsistic uses of language to making such connections, the king's horses and the king's men could have been elsewhere and more gainfully employed. His effrontery was to bring his individual private use of language into the public domain.

An individual's trigger words and expressions for wine – or indeed perfumes or cheeses or any other complex array of sensations – is a proper private use of language. Language used without the need to elude our separateness, free of the pressure of seeking 'the comfort and advantage of communication of thoughts' – a private use of language that revels in the efforts to overcome the limitations of language to express the infinitely subtle experience of our senses.

17
Wine and Words: an empirical approach

Matching wine with words can be a difficult task, particularly if the wine is unfamiliar and the flavour or bouquet elusive. Just how difficult was brought out by a series of experiments Adrienne Lehrer conducted, designed to throw light on the relation between language and the senses.

Three groups took part in the experiments which were a mix of tests and discussions, sometimes beforehand, sometimes afterwards. One group were experts – wine scientists from the Department of Viticulture and Enology at the University of California at Davis. The other two groups were made up mostly of people who enjoyed wine and drank it regularly but did not feel they were particularly knowledgeable.

'In the absence of tests,' Lehrer notes, 'speakers seem to think they are communicating – that they mean the same thing when they use the same words' (Lehrer, 1983: 135). The most striking aspect of her results, however, is the immense variation she brings to light between individuals – experts and non-experts alike – in the ways they link wine and words.

The first task for one of the non-expert groups, for instance, was to describe without conferring the taste, smell and feel in the mouth of three distinct wines. A major factor influencing their choice of language, it turned out, was whether or not they liked the wine. One red wine was described as 'sweet, bubbly . . . flowery, light fizzy feeling in the mouth' by a subject who liked it, and as 'harsh odor, pungent, unpleasant; taste is bitter, sharp' by one who did not.

When conferring was allowed then some convergence did become possible. In one test the group was split into pairs. Each pair had to taste three wines then agree on verbal descriptions for the bouquets/tastes. In most cases the pairs were able to agree with one another on a description which they were then extremely pleased with – as though achieving a consensus with another taster had increased their confidence in their judgement: the private confirmed by being made public. What was significant, however, was just how little agreement there was *between pairs*. Different couples came up with quite different, often conflicting, characterisations of the same wine, each nevertheless supremely confident in the results of their particular joint effort.

The most difficult tests, or at least those where subjects in all three groups generally performed worst, were 'matching' experiments – typically done in twos, one partner tasting and describing three distinct wines, the other then tasting the wines and trying to match them up correctly with their partner's verbal descriptions. Much of the matching for both experts and non-experts was no better than chance.

Though the experts did not shine in Adrienne Lehrer's matching experiments, there were other tests in which they did better than the other groups. Overall, however, her results show that being an expert does not guarantee overcoming the problems inherent in matching wine and words. 'The task of encoding into language the perceptual properties of complex and varied stimuli, such as wines, and subsequently decoding such messages,' she concludes, 'is an extremely difficult one, even for people with great knowledge and experience' (Lehrer, 1983: 129).

Her transcripts of discussions between members of the various groups are particularly illuminating for the light they throw on the public/private mix inherent in wine talk. In this extract, for instance, four members of one of the non-expert groups are trying to characterise an unfamiliar wine, 'Z', so that they will be able to describe it to the others later:

E : Oh, there's something in Z. When you smell it, before you drink it.
W : Yes, I smelled it when I first sat down. You just take a sniff . . .
E : I think burnt rubber.
D : Burnt rubber! . . . I think it smells woody or something.
W : I think it smells perfumy.
E : Woody. I said straw – old . . .
W : Aftersmell of some woodhue.
E : Woody is not bad, it seems.

A :   Reminiscent of a woody perfume.
E :   But only at the first smell.
D :   Vegetable or something organic.
W :   It's organic to me. It smells like 401 labs.
E :   Maybe it's slightly rotten . . . I feel there's a chemical. Chemical seems to be right . . . medicinal. I feel that about this. It's not a natural grape.
W :   Almost plastic.
E :   Straw.

Lehrer, 1983: 170–1

E and *W*, in particular, grope for words mixing their individual associations with reactions to what the others say. In the course of this brief extract *E* moves from 'burnt rubber' to 'woody' to 'old straw' to something 'slightly rotten', 'chemical', 'medicinal' and eventually back to 'straw.' *W* from 'perfumy' through 'woodhue' to the highly idiosyncratic 'like 401 labs' to 'almost plastic'.

At another session a group try different types of comparison in their efforts to characterise the difference between acid and tannin:

E :   It seems to me that acidity and tannin are hard to distinguish.
O :   Yeah, how *do* you distinguish those?
E :   Acidic strikes me as the contrast between grapefruit and milk. Roughly with grapefruity being acidic and milk being flat . . .
O :   What is tannin?
E :   It's an acid, and it's a puckery quality.
O :   Aha!

Without the intonation it is hard to know what *O* intends by his 'Aha!' since he is being told that tannin 'is an acid' in the course of a discussion on how to tell tannin and acid apart. *E* goes on:

E: So astringency or tannin tends to be an unpleasant sharpness. Right? Puckery . . .
R: Persimmons.
E: Acidic isn't necessarily unpleasant. Grapefruit, for instance. But astringency is a sort of unpleasant harshness,

I would say, as contrasted with – just goes down awfully smooth. Velvety, or soft.

O: If you were thinking about, or say you were eating pork or something, wouldn't astringency be a kind of nice thing? Wipe out the grease?

O introduces context, in this instance the context of food, as a relevant and critical factor in deciding how a sensation is to be expressed. *E* concurs: 'Yeah, you'd want something with tannin or acidity. One or the other would do'.

Then a hitherto silent member of the group interposes a third comparison in an attempt to pin the sensation down with words – 'N: Have you ever had a cup of tea that was too strong? Took a mouthful, and it made the inside of your mouth feel dry?' (Lehrer, 1983: 171–2).

Grapefruit, persimmons, strong tea: each used to evoke taste experience, or by contrast: pork and milk. Communal groping towards individual understanding.

Such discussions proved particularly valuable in uncovering the reasons for discrepancies, not only in the words individuals associated with specific sensations, but also in the different links they make, individually, between words:

A: It's bitter to me.

B: It doesn't seem bitter to me.

A: . . . I think it's less bitter than the others but I tend not to like dry wine, so I would probably say that all dry wines are bitter.

(*A* was the only taster who preferred sweet wines to dry ones)

A: . . . perfumy?

B: Not quite perfumy – that's a little bit too sweet. A faint aroma. You know – drier than the other we tasted – and it doesn't have as much of a fruity flavour.

A: I don't think it's fruity . . . but I tend to think it smells perfumy.

B: I don't think the smell is sweet enough to be called perfumy.

A: So perfumy is sweet to you.

B: Yes.

Lehrer, 1983: 84

This discussion makes explicit one of *B*'s intralinguistic links – for him if something is perfumy, it follows that it is sweet – a link *A* does not share.

For his part *B* learns that there is a link for *A* between being dry and being bitter – an intralinguistic link *B* does not share. These are private links now made public. If *A* and *B* keep on using 'perfumy' and 'dry' together they will only converge if they take on board these intralinguistic differences which normally lie hidden.

Another striking result of Adrienne Lehrer's research is the discrepancy it brought to light between the way people perform and the way they believe they perform. The second 'non-expert' group, for instance, met over an eight-month period during which their performance in the objective tests showed little significant improvement. Members of this group nevertheless *felt* they had learnt a lot and could use words more precisely and consistently. 'No one ever made a remark on the order of "I'll describe this wine as cheesy and sullen, since none of these words means anything anyhow",' Adrienne Lehrer commented (Lehrer, 1983: 112).

On the contrary, she found them generally keen to learn 'proper' wine terminology, often apologetic when they felt they were getting things wrong. They had found their discussions informative, they wanted to do better. Ironically perhaps, they continued to believe there was a correct way of using wine terms in spite of taking part in experiments which illustrated the limitations inherent in such a view.

18

Feeling We Understand

Adrienne Lehrer reported that during discussion sessions subjects often described wines by comparing them with other substances whose tastes and smells the others might know. Sometimes it was other wines or liquors; sometimes quite different substances: *'burlap, cheese, crabapples, dill, fish, formaldehyde, Listerine, medicine, mutton, persimmons, quinine, raisins, rancid butter, soy sauce, turkey and wheat'*.

'Even more distant associations were observed,' she says, 'such as descriptions of wine as being *autumnal, sexy, opulent or ragged*' (Lehrer, 1983: 106).

What the experimenting tasters were doing, in effect, was testing whether their personal 'trigger words' also worked for others. This is language used to tap another's sensory memory, one person saying that this wine has a hint of soy sauce in its flavour, for instance, or that one a whiff of formaldehyde in its bouquet, in the hope that another on tasting will make the connection too.

If it works, if the same connections are made, a special kind of convergence has been achieved, not so much between speaker and hearer meanings for the same words as between speaker and hearer associations of smells and tastes and language.

Sometimes it seems to work easily. Suppose you were set the task of tasting three white wines and matching them with three verbal descriptions provided by another taster. One description mentions 'grapefruit'. One of the wines reminds you unmistakably of grapefruit and you match correctly.

All this may show, however, is that you and your tasting partner happen to share similar tastes. Adrienne Lehrer's subjects gradually learnt whose tastes they shared and thus whose palates they could trust. She says:

This is not to say that some individuals were recognised by the rest as experts and trustworthy. Rather, subjects to some extent filtered descriptions on the basis of the speaker. If one subject preferred heavy tannic wines, those subjects who disliked that type of wine would apparently give less weight to the speaker's description.

Lehrer, 1983: 112

To those who have never been challenged to translate an elusive taste into words, some of the comparisons her subjects came up with may seem far-fetched: It is not immediately obvious after all how 'soy sauce' or 'turkey' or 'rancid butter' could evoke the flavour or the bouquet of a wine.

Difficult though it may be, however, it is still easier than trying to imagine an 'autumnal' or a 'sexy' or a 'ragged' wine. 'Soy sauce' and 'turkey' and 'rancid butter' are at least related to actual physical substances with distinctive smells and tastes to provide some kind of 'settled standard in Nature to rectify and adjust' their meanings by.

Not so 'autumnal' or 'sexy' or 'ragged'. At the risk of appearing pedestrian, could a wine really have an 'autumnal' taste or a 'sexy' bouquet or a 'ragged' one? Or rather, if one particular taster says it does, how likely is it that such descriptions would arouse comparable associations for another?

The pedestrian answer is probably 'not very likely'. Yet this is not the whole story. If we were to taste the wine, particularly in the right company, we might well *feel* we understood what the speaker meant when he called it 'autumnal' or 'sexy' or 'ragged'. We could still have the sense we knew what he was getting at even if we could not say what it was.

Fantasy can and often does play a role in the way we match what we feel and what we say. An eighteen-year-old who had done badly in his A-levels was talking to a journalist about school:

> If I try to analyse or look at things more deeply . . . it gets like a web or muddle . . . I get to the end of a sentence, my mind slips away, then I've forgotten what I've written. So I read it again and then I can't remember what I've written. So I read it again and then I can't remember what I was thinking about any-way . . . 'What does your head feel like?' . . . Like I could take it off and put it on the desk and let it go to sleep. Like I've been doing in lessons for years and years.

Kee, 1984

Except, of course, that he hadn't been taking off his head and putting it on the desk for years and years. How could he? But this does not prevent us – if we are sympathetic and make the necessary effort – *feeling* we understand from his words something of the sensations he is talking about. Not precisely. Precision and exactness have no place in talk about sensation. But 'sort of', 'more or less', which is often the closest to convergence we can get.

Our fantasies can be of all kinds. Humorous sometimes: this writer was talking about tracking down a rat that had got trapped under the floorboards: 'I shall never forget the smell, which I can only describe as grey and suggestive of very old witches' (Hart-Davis, 1986).

No matter that no one could ever have actually smelled 'very old witches': the words can touch off a feeling we understand. Appeal to our imagination. Even if we could not say precisely what it was we imagine.

The best poets and playwrights and novelists are skilled at using words to excite in us a keen sense of place or person, feeling or emotion. Consider Caliban's lyrical account of his island in *The Tempest*:

> Be not afeard: the isle is full of noises,
> Sounds, and sweet airs, that give delight, and hurt not.
> Sometimes a thousand twangling instruments
> Will hum about mine ears; and sometimes voices,
> That, if I then had waked after long sleep,
> Will make me sleep again; and then, in dreaming,
> The clouds, methought, would open and show riches
> Ready to drop upon me; that, when I waked,
> I cried to dream again.

> (3.ii.)

No cartographer, however skilled, could begin to draw a map from Caliban's words. Precision and exactness have no place when language is used to arouse impressions, sensations, feelings. Idyllic, dream-like, Caliban's isle is no specific place; we are each of us as hearers free to understand him as we will. Free, too, to leave our understanding blurred and shadowy: feeling we understand without being able to put our understanding into words.

This shadowy sense of knowing is common when we read novels and come to feel familiar with the characters. We have a sense of them which we could not necessarily make precise but we know we have it all the same. It can hit us abruptly if the book is made into a film or television serial. The actors can seem quite wrong – not corresponding at all to our sense of the characters. We can feel this, even if we could not express at all clearly what our sense of them was.

On a different plane, but no less effective sometimes, advertising copywriters choose their words expressly to lure us, willingly, into the realms of fantasy. When they are selling luxuries in particular: fast cars, beauty products, holidays on sun-soaked, far-away beaches.

One such luxury is perfume. Normally those selling perfumes do not even try to describe them directly. Any such attempt would be almost certainly doomed to failure, as this journalist's description of a new perfume, Diva, shows:

> Diva is an innovative amber-warm and vibrantly floral fragrance, with a quality that lasts without changing radically when you wear it. At the base is a deep amber note which influences the entire fragrance. Mysore sandalwood, patchouli, and oak-moss lend it a woody crispness. The body notes are extremely rich florals chosen to enhance the amber note. Turkish rose, honeyed Moroccan rose, Florentine iris, narcissus and Egyptian jasmine form a warm bouquet which is headed by Indian tuberose . . . aromatic cardamom, fresh mandarin and ylang ylang. All this blends beautifully with not a note out of place.
>
> Bentley, 1986

Though she has listed the various elements of the perfume faithfully enough, the parts, as with faces, do not readily add up to a recognisable whole.

Perfumes are as difficult as wines to translate into words. Advertisers generally avoid the problem by combining words and pictures to excite, not the smell of a particular perfume so much as the effect of wearing it: *Rive Gauche*, for example: 'Le parfum des femmes imprévisibles.'

Or sometimes the lifestyle associated with wearing it: *parfum d'Hermès*:

> She wears a silk scarf by Hermès, but with jeans or a wind-jammer . . . She adores champagne but wouldn't dream of drinking it at Christmas . . . She loves tradition, but likes to

stand out in a crowd. She is several women, yet she is unique. Parfum d'Hermès is her perfume.

Similarly for *Royal Secret* from Monteil:

> Jetting off to the exotic east, during a glamorous night in a foreign capital, cushioned in the luxury of a limousine, Royal Secret will be your partner. And for the one who loves you, its rich fragrance embodies the warmth of your personality.

Advertisements for perfumes rarely give any but the broadest hints as to the actual smell of the perfume itself. Yet this does not prevent women attracted by the promised effect *feeling* they know the perfume without even smelling it at all.

The use of language by creative writers or advertisers to excite a response in readers or potential buyers is a skilled and studied way with words. Composing can take time, draft after draft, discussion after discussion. Not everyone can do it. Nor does it always work.

Few of us, for instance, asked for an instant reaction are capable on the spot of flights of imagination in matching what we have experienced with words. Stephen Waldorf, who was shot accidentally by the police, was asked by reporters to talk about the experience:

> I don't know how one talks about that sort of pain. I don't know what the words are. It's the sort of pain that when I was hit over the head with a gun, I didn't even feel it. I thought I was paralysed in my legs.

A woman whose son vanished at sea was told that a roll of film had been found on a beach recording his last moments: 'It came as rather a shock. It is a difficult emotion to put into words'.

In less dramatic circumstances, too, we can find ourselves groping for words that elude us. We *feel* we know what we mean, it can be vivid to us, the way someone behaves, the sense of a place, the intuition that something is wrong, or that something has changed. But when we try and say what we are sure we know, the words seem too simple for the complexity of the feeling. An old man who had worked in one of the Colleges of Cambridge University in the 1930s and 1940s was trying to express what was so different about 'the old days': 'You can't explain really the difference. You can say it one way and you can say it another, but you can't make anything now of what it was like then'.

He had written to one of the students he had known in the past: 'I wrote to this man and told him how the College was changed and everything . . . I explained everything to him . . . I wrote two letters to him . . . '

'What did you say?'

'Well, I told him how it was all completely different'.

Christine Piff lost part of her face including her left eye through a rare form of cancer. In her book *Let's Face It* she described in a down-to-earth way what happened to her. Some of the stranger sensations caused by the treatment she had to undergo nevertheless defeated her:

The infection in my orbit [the space where her eye had been] was persistent, to say the least. . . Then, at my next session with Mr Wallace, he produced a magic spray.

'This will help to get rid of the infection', he said, as he shook the aerosol can. I lacked confidence. It was bad enough having the orbit cleaned, let alone have an aerosol sprayed into it. Oh, well, grit your teeth and here we go.

The sensation I felt is indescribable.

'If I fall on the floor with my legs and arms in the air twitching like mad, you'll know I'm done for'.

Piff, 1986: 91–2

A girl talked about the way she felt during one of her A-level examinations: 'Then about half an hour before the end, I stopped. I couldn't go on. It was terrible: a weird feeling, un-nameable'.

But then she made an effort of the imagination: 'It's as if you were on a big wheel and you can just see the sea and your stomach's turning and you think you're going to go flying out into it' (Kee, 1984).

This is usually as far as we can succeed in getting others to converge on what we have experienced: 'It's as if . . . ', 'It's just like . . . '. More often than not we cannot even do that: 'No, I can't describe it. I don't know what the words are'.

The potential is there in language, right enough, but we cannot always realise it. For even if we find the words, we cannot guarantee that others will make the necessary effort to understand.

And even if they try, even if they *feel* they know what we are saying, this is likely to be at least in part an illusion.

Early man, in a fictional form depicted in William Golding's extraordinary and haunting book, *The Inheritors*, had a capacity to communicate without words:

> Lok yearned suddenly for the mindless peace of their accord. He put his fit of temper on one side and crept back to the fire, pretending to be very miserable so that they pretended to comfort him. Then there was silence again and one mind or no mind in the overhang.
>
> Quite without warning, all the people shared a picture inside their heads. This was a picture of Mal, seeming a little removed from them, illuminated, sharply defined in all his gaunt misery. They saw not only Mal's body but the slow pictures that were waxing and waning in his head. One above all was displacing the others, dawning through the cloudy arguments and doubts and conjectures until they knew what it was he was thinking with such dull conviction.
>
> 'Tomorrow or the day after, I shall die'.
>
> Golding, 1961: 38–9

We still have this capacity, each of us with a chosen few. We can know what others are thinking, occasionally. Indeed it is another of the ironies of language that some communication can work most successfully without words at all.

19
Language and Emotion

'We are inclined to say that when we communicate a feeling to
someone, something which can never be known happens at the
other end.'

Wittgenstein

Words, however inadequate, are nevertheless one of the most
important ways we share emotions and feelings and reactions
with others. As is silence: 'You're very quiet. Are you all right?'
Some silences feel brooding and ominous, just as others feel
comfortable and warm.

Sometimes we are silent because we do not quite know how we
feel, whether what is happening inside counts as 'all right' or not.
Emotions are often tangled; they do not bubble up, neatly labelled
with suitable words. We feel independently of whether we could
say more than grossly what it is that we feel.

It is often easier, for instance, to explain why we are in a
particular mood than what kind of mood it is. 'How do you feel?'
'Well, the dog's just been sick on the carpet/I've been made
redundant/the kids are playing up . . .'

In so doing we are leaning heavily on the public, shared, side of
human experience, assuming – though we cannot be certain –
that our hearer would feel very much as we do if they had been
made redundant or their kids were playing up or their dog had
been sick yet again.

We have little choice but to be indirect since language serves us
badly when it comes to describing directly what is going on
inside. The words we use to say we are 'fine' or 'excited' or
'depressed' or 'fed up' serve millions of 'excited' or 'fed up' people
who are excited or fed up more or less, in countless different ways.

The words are public, shared, common to all of us, revealing no
more than grossly the private moods and emotions we separately
experience. If I say 'I'm really depressed', what I mean by

133

depressed is the emotional state I am in. Whatever that state is, I am calling it 'depressed'. In a sense, my meaning as speaker is that I feel the way I feel.

This is not to say, though, that my words will be meaningless to a hearer who should understand that I am down rather than up, for instance, dejected rather than cheerful. If my tone is flat or I seem generally listless, this may offer some further clue as to just how down or dejected I am. But that is all – words, no more than crude 'labels' for what may be complex states of feeling, clues as to the broad sweep of what I feel – good or bad, positive or negative. Convergence between our separate meanings as speaker and hearer would be unlikely to be close. Or rather, if we were converging, how could we know that we were?

*   *   *

Some talk is not so much about feelings as to relieve feelings. 'Some people just have an awful lot to say', said one marriage guidance counsellor. 'Things have got too much for them, so they talk on and on, get everything out and present it to the counsellor as a package, saying, there it is, now you do something about it'.

'I don't think they see us to begin with', another counsellor commented. 'They know we're there but that's about all. I don't think they hear us either'. 'Often when people first come to us,' a social worker said, 'They use us as a sounding board. We try to let them get things off their chests'.

We are all familiar with this use of language to get things off one's chest, off one's mind, out of one's system, the use of language to bring into the open what has been festering inside. Saying it aloud can be a valuable part of the process of making the private public, enabling us to escape some of the aloneness of overwhelming feeling, to start to forge some sense of what seems without sense.

When using language is like opening an escape valve, allowing into the open feelings built up inside, a hearer may better understand the *fact* of the feelings behind the words than the precise nature of the feelings themselves. When words are being used to express strong emotion, communication – convergence between speaker and hearer meanings – may not even be the primary aim at all. Listening to the worst of an individual's distress can sometimes mean accepting the role of hearer to a speaker not particularly concerned whether you understand or not.

Language to relieve, and sometimes to understand better our tangled feelings is not always face to face. Writing too can help to heal. Janet Taylor lost her teenage daughter, Brigie, after a short and sudden illness:

> I remember the moment when I realised I would have to write about my daughter – I knew that the amazing transformation in our lively girl and our new closeness around her must be kept fresh in the family memory . . . After she died it became vital to me to get down on paper a brief chronology of everything that has happened in the three months of her illness . . . I began to feel guilty, though, as I kept badgering others in the family, asking them to relive particular incidents, bringing painful memories to the surface again when they were struggling to cope with ordinary life after such an intense time.

She began to write: 'weeping . . . late into the night . . .By January, just over a year after Brigie had died, I was working at fever-pitch, absorbed and *happy* I realised with a shock'.

As she wrote on the focus began to change:

> As the words poured out, they were not simply to the family. It had become essential to communicate and share the goodness we had received through the pain . . . I had no time to think about the implications of the change of focus. I could just go on and on, stopping late at night only when totally exhausted, falling asleep with the words of the last sentence pounding in my brain and waking a few hours later with them rearranging themselves and demanding to be rewritten . . . There was nothing else that I wanted to do. Although I was working very fast, I did not want the end to come: it was just as if Brigie were dying all over again, but it was the intense desire to communicate and share that kept pushing me on, and this tempered the sadness of the ending.
>
> Taylor, 1984

For Janet Taylor, writing some time after her daughter died, the initial relief of making the private public turned to a positive desire to engage with others and share. Under the immediate impact of shock or pain, however, the force of strong emotion can often make us inarticulate.

Nancy Banks Smith commented on the way television reported the fire which engulfed Bradford City's packed Valley Stadium one Saturday afternoon during a match:

> People say on such occasions that there are no words to describe it . . . They underrate English but it does seem as if the moment burns away everything but the bones of the language, leaving only the simplest, shortest words, and few of them.

She gave an illustration: 'A biggish, stunned looking chap was asked what he saw: "I see a bloke in there . . . you know, I see a bloke in there, where he was, in flames. What can you say? You can't say any more, can you?"' (Banks Smith, 1985).

'They underrate English'. In a sense she is right. Words do not fail us because there are no words. On the contrary, in calmer moments people can call upon the rich resources of their language to produce eloquent and moving accounts of what they saw or felt. But rarely at the time. Rarely when they are still choked with emotion, participants in the drama being enacted around them. It would be different if they were not closely involved, if instead they were observers, sympathetic but essentially detached. As observers they might more readily find words for feelings not so strongly felt.

Sometimes the need to relieve our feelings by talk can last long after the initial shock. Satya Schofield worked as a counsellor at a centre set up to help distressed survivors of the Bradford football stadium fire. A year after the tragedy she talked to Tony Parker:

> Many people . . . seem to feel there's a stigma attached to not being able to cope themselves with their own emotions and thoughts. They feel by now they ought to have got over it – sometimes it's almost as if they want permission to still be talking about the subject. But if they can, when they do, it's a healing process, there's no doubt at all about that.
>
> Parker, 1986

There is at the same time the danger that professionals – counsellors, social workers and the like – will overrate the value of the kind of talk that brings emotional relief. Rees and Wallace

(1982) gave this assessment of the benefits of talking in social work:

> talking is praised as being valuable by clients mainly due to the emotional relief they experience – and that is all. Few clients perceive any other real benefits in 'just talking'. A few 'appreciate the opportunity of talking which can provide them with a new perspective on, and insight into, themselves . . . ' But for the rest: 'They experience relief, but then want something more'.

*　　*　　*

Strong emotion does not just affect what we are able to say, it can affect equally what we hear, the way we understand what other people say. In the grip of resentment or bitterness or anger, we are so much more likely to be locked into our own perspective, interpret what others say from our own standpoint. This can have practical consequences, provoking quarrels and misunderstandings, divergence rather than convergence.

Advisers such as lawyers or social workers, for instance, are sometimes confronted with clients who consult them still choked with overwhelming bitterness or anger or grief. So common is this in divorce or child custody cases that a group of British lawyers committed to a conciliatory approach to family disputes, the Solicitors' Family Law Society, organised a seminar on 'the first interview' largely devoted to problems of coping with distressed clients.

Often such clients 'only hear what they want to hear', said solicitor Joan Rubenstein, who is also a psychotherapist. Not deliberately or wilfully, but rather because their emotion so colours their hearer meaning for the lawyer's words that convergence with his speaker meaning is very difficult to achieve.

Some of the lawyers present – mostly women – said they did not even try to advise such clients in the early stages but simply let them talk themselves into a calmer state. Such an approach, however, is inevitably time-consuming – others could not see how it was practicable to allow clients on Legal Aid the time that would be required.

'They only hear what they want to hear' is a simple phrase for a complex state. Stress and emotion can lock us into our own perspective, make us hear others say what we already believe they mean. Distressed clients can present professional givers of advice with particularly difficult problems. 'If clients come in wanting to hear certain things,' Joan Rubenstein warned the lawyers attending the 'first interview' seminar, 'they may go away *believing* they have heard those things'. The result could be that they take action which is against their own interest in the end.

One solution suggested – by no means foolproof – was to check carefully and explicitly that clients have understood what was being said. Some lawyers said they did this by making sure they wrote to the client straight after the interview laying out in detail what they believed had been established. This had the advantage both of covering them in case of complaint, and of allowing any discrepancy between what they had said and what the client had understood to come to light.

Though they had no ready solutions, these were nevertheless lawyers already conscious to different degrees of the potential problems posed by an unthinking use of language in emotionally-charged situations. Not all professional advisers, however, are so concerned. Many lawyers, for instance, see their professional role as one of dispensing legal advice and representing clients without undue concern for their emotional state.

This robust approach seems perfectly justifiable on the face of it. Solicitors are, after all, experts in the law; few are psychotherapists; few have any special skills in dealing with distress.

Its main flaw, though, lies in its view of what constitutes giving advice. When lawyers advise they do so in words. They say or write words that for them express the advice they judge appropriate: 'The best course would be for you to do this' or 'The house will have to be sold unless you do that'. They know what advice they are giving. Their words have a clear enough speaker meaning.

Saying the words that express advice is, however, only one side of advising. Advice given is not necessarily advice received. The adviser's words will have a second meaning, the hearer meaning, the client's meaning. A client's meaning which in straightforward cases *may* converge quite closely with that of the lawyer. Advice successfully given. A client's meaning equally which may diverge from the lawyer's – coloured by hope or guilt, distress or bitterness. Advice given but not received.

Sensitive lawyers are aware of the dangers of divergence though they may not use such terms. They see it as part of their professional duty to take some responsibility for trying to improve convergence; they repeat, rephrase, ask, check. Others, though, are content with simply saying the words. 'I told him what he ought to do. The idiot simply took no notice'.

Advising is more complex than we sometimes realise. The problems it poses bring out some of the basic limitations of language: the way words can allow us to go through the motions of communicating when in effect no contact takes place. As teachers teach but students do not necessarily learn, so advisers advise but those who consult them are not necessarily advised.

On his side the adviser – who may be a lawyer, but who could equally well be a social worker, for instance, or a doctor – can say what for him are the right words. But if the person advised is stuck fast in his own perspective, if he is making assumptions the adviser does not know about, if he is emotionally battered, unable to take in what he hears, if he is agitated, or depressed, or vengeful or bitter, then the advice may hang in the air, or be understood in a quite distorted version.

The problem is that advisers are, in the end, as trapped within their own heads as the rest of us, not knowing, not able to know for certain what clients have understood. For lawyers this can present special difficulties in that, though they explain matters and give advice, in the end they are bound by their client's instructions. They do what their client wants them to do – making it doubly important both that they have understood their client's story properly, and that the client understands his options.

Major J. G. R. Allen's comments in his 1985 *Report of the Lay Observer*, on complaints against solicitors, suggest that convergence of meaning between solicitor and client has not always been close enough:

> Another frequent cause of complaint . . . is the solicitor's failure to explain matters in terms which his clients can understand: not all solicitors seem sufficiently to realise that almost identical sets of circumstances require quite different approaches to explanation for different types of client.
>
> *Lay Observer's Report*, 1985: 10

More specifically on divorce cases, he comments in an earlier Report:

A relatively high proportion of them [complaints] have been against solicitors acting for the other party and the [Law] Society has very seldom been able to investigate them because the action complained of may well have been taken on the specific instructions of the solicitor's client with which the solicitor must comply unless they are clearly improper. Moreover, a solicitor is entitled to believe what his client tells him, unless he has a clear indication that it is untrue.

Lay Observer's Report, 1984: 10

But if clients are in a state only 'to hear what they want to hear' it cannot always be easy for solicitors to know what is true and what is wishful thinking. They can of course look for clues in what is said, in tone of voice, whether the client seems to be paying attention, how he looks, how he acts – the so-called 'body language', which can be more difficult to read than we are sometimes led to believe.

But they can still be wrong. As one adviser, a social worker this time, acknowledged:

Sometimes people seem to be listening, but they're not really taking in what you're saying. They're just going through the motions. Sometimes they just want to please you. To them you may be a figure of authority. They may be saying what they think you want.

Often, though, advisers are only too aware of the difficulties they face: 'The worst clients of all are teachers', one lawyer said:

They're used to being in authority and they're not used to being questioned. They resent having to get advice. They want to know everything, all the legal details, then they get books on it and read it all up, then they find they can't take it all in. They won't necessarily tell you the problem at all – they think they're solving it themselves if you'll just give them a bit of information. In the end they are most likely to ignore what you've said.

*   *   *

Marriage guidance counsellors also deal regularly with clients beset by strong and complex feelings. Unlike lawyers they may see warring spouses together in an attempt to help them resolve their difficulties. 'People are often afraid of hearing what they don't want to know', one counsellor said. Part of only 'hearing what you want to hear' is avoiding hearing what you do not:

> The wife who suspects her husband of having another woman, for instance, may be in a turmoil. She wants to know and is afraid to know at the same time. So she might challenge him, but then not give him the chance to reply. She might change the subject or interrupt at the crucial moment or involve us in some diversionary tactic. People have all manner of devious means of preventing their partner saying what they don't want to hear.

This is another twist to the way emotion affects our use of language – a sort of separation of words from their 'terrain'. The woman who uses diversionary tactics to prevent particular words being spoken knows their meaning even if they are not said. She knows the meaning of what her husband would say – *if* he said it. Yet so long as he does not actually say it, so long as his unfaithfulness is not expressed in words, it remains possible for her to shut her eyes to it. Language used to foster an illusion. Except that if she closes her eyes to the problem, it does not go away, so she asks him again.

Talking of the problems of communicating with troubled children who had spent a lot of their young lives in care, children already battered by life, a social worker commented: 'Sometimes they chatter non-stop as a way of avoiding what *you* want to talk to them about'. One sort of language used as a barrier to block out another sort that may cause pain.

Counsellors whose job it is to try and help distressed and troubled clients become accustomed to these diverse uses of talk. Talk for the benefit of the talker. Talk where feeling and emotion cloud convergence.

We have all at some time or another used language to help us hide what we feel rather than reveal an inner ache. It is one of the many paradoxes inherent in language that it serves us better to cover up our feelings than to express what we truly feel.

Part III
The Language of Reflection

'The steps are laid down by the prophet who says, "Unless you believe, you shall not understand."'

St Augustine, *De Libero Arbitrio*

20
Taking Part and Standing Back

'Seattle. Jimi Hendrix came from here. And there's the hotel where Led Zeppelin tied up a girl and did some fishing from their bedroom window, or something. It was funny three years later to go back with my own band and fish from the same windows of the Edgewater Inn. From observer to participant.'

Bob Geldof, *Is That It?*

Virtually unnoticed, our use of language reflects two roles we move between throughout our lives. One is the role of PARTICIPANT, taking part in what is going on around us, absorbed, involved, the other the role of OBSERVER, standing back, taking stock, assessing and explaining ourselves and others.

Sometimes we play both parts at once, 'participating' publicly, on the outside, while privately, on the inside, 'observing', judging, remaining detached.

When words are an integral part of what we are doing, when, for instance, we argue or complain, request or persuade, enthuse or criticise, then we are using language primarily as 'participants'.

When we are in the midst of a full-scale row with someone, we are both 'participants'. When we say what we say, yell what we yell, spurred on by anger or bitterness or indignation, we are involved, bound up in what is happening. When we chair a meeting we are 'participants', playing a role in a tiny real-life drama, influencing by what we say, how and when we say it, what we do not say, the way the drama is enacted. When we return to a shop with a toaster that will not toast or a pair of shoes that fell apart on first wearing, we are 'participants', poised to present the evidence and negotiate compensation.

When at other times we use language to reflect or consider, mull things over, talk them through, reconstruct what happened to us

145

as 'participants', then we are primarily 'observers'. Using language to stand back, take stock, explain ourselves after the event.

At the end of the day, for instance, running over what has happened to us, reliving whatever crossed us, whatever threatened us, whatever moved us, we become 'observers', using language to give an account, or tell ourselves a story that makes whatever it was that happened less unintelligible, less wounding, less alien.

Like the part-private, part-public nature of meaning, the distinction between using language as a 'participant' and as an 'observer' is a rough-and-ready one. Our ordinary use of language is part-participant/part-observer, one or other dominant at any one time, talk a constant ebb and flow between the two.

Rough and ready though it may be, however, the participant/observer distinction nevertheless throws new light on the ends served by language – traditionally, the functions of language.

Most current analyses of language functions can be traced back 50 years to Karl Bühler's *Sprachtheorie* (1934). Bühler's analysis of the functions of language was linked to a view, widely-held in his time, of an utterance as the focus of a drama in which there were three elements: a speaker, a hearer and a state-of-affairs to which, it was held, the utterance referred.

Simplifying considerably, utterances were classified according to whether they primarily *described* the state-of-affairs, *expressed* the speaker's attitude to the state-of-affairs or *appealed to* the hearer to participate in the state-of-affairs. So 'Max is on the phone' would be primarily 'descriptive', 'Good old Max', primarily 'expressive' and 'Get me a drink, Max, please', primarily 'appellative'.

Bühler's three-way classification was later modified and extended, most notably by the eminent linguist, Roman Jakobson, who added three further functions: the 'phatic' – talk to oil the wheels of society; the 'poetic', the creative use of language and the 'metalinguistic', language used to talk about language. Nowadays most linguists assume three more or less distinguishable functions: the 'descriptive' or 'referential'; the 'expressive' and the 'social'. Some prefer a two-way classification: the 'referential' and the 'interpersonal'.

Over the years linguists, philosophers and anthropologists have disagreed as to whether the 'descriptive' or 'referential' role of language – language used to describe or give information about a state-of-affairs – is more basic than the other roles. One of the reasons it has been accorded so much importance is that it has been largely taken for granted that 'the world' exists 'out there' to be described. There appears to have been a tacit assumption within the Bühler tradition that neutral, unmarked descriptions of 'states-of-affairs', independent of the views of different observers, are possible. For many the chief end of language is to provide such descriptions.

Looking at language as serving our ends as 'participants' or 'observers' is quite distinct from the Bühler tradition. The assumption underlying the participant/observer distinction is that there is no external vantage point from which speakers and hearers can use language to describe or refer to independently existing states-of-affairs. Either they are participating in, and thereby creating the state-of-affairs, or else they are standing back, taking stock, reconstructing, assessing, judging from their own vantage point what has taken place.

An important consequence of keeping in mind the participant/observer distinction is that it discourages us from expecting to find a neat, objective match between language and the world.

Having a language with an observer dimension means that we can not only take part in the activities of the world but also recall, relive and reconstruct their impact on us. There can be no guarantee, however, that each one of us will recall and relive and reconstruct even the 'same' activities in the same way.

Though observer language has its limitations, it is nevertheless vital to us. More so perhaps than we often realise. If we could not talk things over, tell stories, relive experience, revise our reactions, reconsider, how could we even begin to make sense of what we undergo?

Observer language allows us to create what we sometimes call our 'view of the world' which is less a single view than a collection of views which are not necessarily coherent or consistent. If these views stray too far from what we cheerfully call 'reality' they are perhaps better described as fantasies about the world – observer language allows us to create indifferently 'views of the world' or a collection of fantasies, worlds we wished existed.

Creating views – or fantasies – about the world, taking a perspective, putting a construction on what we experience – these are the distinctive elements of the 'observer' use of language. The side of language that seems uniquely human.

Animal languages, as far as we can tell, are solely participant languages, lacking an 'observer' dimension. Animals act and interact in the immediate about the immediate, their systems of communication apparently tied to the experience of the moment. A chaffinch, for instance, may chirp a particular, identifiable series of notes to warn off an invading neighbour from its territory. Back at the nest, however, the same bird would not, could not as far as we know, reflect on what it had done, discuss with its mate whether, given the circumstances, it had acted wisely, wonder whether the neighbour it had frightened off might be offended, even hurt, mull over its own rather agressive behaviour, conjure with new, different lines of conduct, suppose, imagine . . .

Could not, in effect, do all the kinds of things humans using language as 'observers' do constantly in their efforts to make the world less unintelligible to themselves, to diminish their sense of confusion.

This is not to deny that there are similarities between human and animal languages. Darwin, in *The Descent of Man*, went to considerable lengths to narrow the gap. He drew attention to the characteristics both systems of communication have in common: both have, for instance, well-understood ways of expressing anger, desire, dominance, territorial rights, ownership, mutual regard and affection.

Darwin was, of course, partly right. There is a great deal in common between the ways animals communicate and the participant side of human language, words used to express our immediate response to the world, more often than not, part of a mingled chain of talk and action.

Yet when it matters the differences are more remarkable than the similarities. Lacking an observer use of language, animals have, as far as we can tell, only one life to live, a 'participant' life. For us, moving between 'observer' and 'participant' roles, language opens up an infinite range of lives to consider. All the domains, past and future, keyed by: 'If only I had . . . ' 'Maybe we should . . . ' 'What if we did . . . ' 'It might be better if . . . ' and so on, *ad infinitum*.

More than 100 years after Darwin's *The Descent of Man*, Jane Goodall, a dedicated student of chimpanzees in the wild in Tanzania, remarked of chimps in an interview with Polly Toynbee:

They show us how unique we are: The more I find close similarities with us, the more I realise too how great the gulf is between us. They have no moral sense: in chimp society only might is right. They have no concepts for past and future, and without speech their language is limited. But this tells us also what is important about being human.

Toynbee, 1986

The great gulf Jane Goodall noted is reflected sharply in the human ability to shift from being participants to being observers, reflecting on what has happened, speculating on what may happen, reconstructing the past, shaping the future, elaborating events in recall, exaggerating them, revising our initial reaction – all this, whether we use it wisely or not, firmly sets us apart.

Since observer language is so important, allowing us to explore our experience, channel our emotions, gain some insight into our participant behaviour, it is remarkable we do not value it more. Wittgenstein once commented on the way:

the aspects of things that are most important for us are hidden because of their simplicity and familiarity. (One is unable to notice something – because it is always before one's eyes.) The real foundations of his enquiry do not strike a man at all, unless *that* fact has at some time struck him – And this means: we fail to be struck by what, once seen, is most striking and powerful.

Wittgenstein, 1953: 129

One way of beginning to notice the obvious is to try and imagine what life would be like without it, without the ability to switch to an 'observer' role, how it would be to be trapped in the immediate, always a 'participant'.

William Golding made that imaginative effort in *The Inheritors* where he created a group of characters, the earliest humans, struggling to develop a language congruent with their experience. Through an exchange between two of them, Lok, the first clown, and Fa, a no-nonsense mother, we catch a glimpse of tool-using creatures close to us in spirit but, in Lok's case at least, almost wholly confined to using language for the immediate.

In the first part of the novel the group have trekked from their winter quarters to where they spend the summer, high in the forests. One day Lok and Fa, foraging at some distance from their new quarters in an overhang by a fall, come across an open space rich in their staple food: young, fat, white shoots. Together they attack the banquet from the edge:

> Side by side they concentrated on the circle, eating in. There was so much that they talked as they ate, brief ejaculations of pleasure and excitement, there was so much that for a while they ceased to feel famished and were only hungry.
>
> Golding, 1961: 48–9

Once they are replete, Fa tries, slowly and with difficulty, to imagine another state of affairs, to talk, not as they have been talking as they ate, as 'participants', but as an 'observer':

> Lok belched at the patch and looked at it affectionately.
> 'This is a good place'.
> Fa frowned and munched.
> 'If the patch were nearer – '
> She swallowed her mouthful with a gulp.
> 'I have a picture. The good food is growing. Not here. It is growing by the fall'.
> Lok laughed at her.
> 'No plant like this grows near the fall!'
> Fa put her hands wide apart, watching Lok all the time. Then she began to bring them together. But though the tilt of her head, the eyebrows moved slightly up and apart, asked a question she had no words with which to define it. She tried again.
> 'But if – See this picture. The overhang and the fire is down here'.
> Lok lifted his face away from his mouth and laughed.
> 'This place is down here. And the overhang and the fire is there'.
> He broke off more shoots, stuffed them into his mouth and went on eating. He looked into the clearer sunlight and read the signs of the day. Presently Fa forgot her picture and stood up.
>
> Golding, 1961: 49–50

Thus it was that Fa's picture, Fa's effort to conceive of farming, to imagine the art and practice of growing food: 'The good food . . .

is growing by the fall' was summarily rejected by the simple
'commonsense' of Lok: the shoots were here; the summer quarters
were somewhere over there; and that was that.

Yet Lok, the 'participant', had a strength Fa lacked. Lok, trapped
almost wholly in the immediate, could as a consequence, read the
signs of the day particularly well:

> He blew out air through his nose suddenly, then breathed in.
> Delicately he sampled this air, drawing a stream into his nostrils
> and allowing it to remain there till his blood had warmed it and
> the scent was accessible. He performed miracles of perception in
> the cavern of his nose. The scent was the smallest possible trace.
> Lok, if he had been capable of such comparisons, might have
> wondered whether the trace was a real scent or only the memory
> of one. So faint and stale was the scent that when he looked his
> question at Fa she did not understand him. He breathed the
> word at her.
> 'Honey?'

Golding, 1961: 50

Lok may not follow Fa's striving to use language as an observer,
to imagine and communicate a different order of things, where
they were farmers as well as foragers, but he can respond with
subtle discrimination to the immediate – and articulate what he
finds.

One of the reasons we may take 'observer' language so much for
granted, why it requires such imaginative effort to see its significance, may be that we use it, more often than not, in quite
ordinary, mundane situations. Consider how, for instance, in the
evening, families and others who live together talk over or tell
stories about the events of the day. Through 'observer' language
they are able to relive almost effortlessly what they have already
lived – only now with a measure of detachment that may open up
the possibility of setting those experiences in a new and different
light.

Take the case of a parent at home looking after young children.
She – for the housebound parent is still more likely to be the
mother – may be only barely aware of the liberating and cathartic
effect of recounting to her partner the events of the day.

As an 'observer', after the event, she is free from the demands of
the actual day itself when as a 'participant' she was all the time

having to act or decide. The need to act, to take decisions, stamp the participant role. In participating in her children's day, she would have used language to direct, persuade, cajole, warn, help, comfort, distract. After the event, as an 'observer', reflecting on the day, she can use language to interpret and comment on events, to embroider if she chooses, free from any pressure to engage.

In this, much idealised, case 'observer' language is being used instinctively and happily to relax and liberate from the cares of the day. Her partner, too, is free to listen in an 'observer' spirit, hearing the stories of minor disasters narrowly averted, small successes fleetingly achieved, reacting without the need to act.

Businesswoman Judith Davenport describes the strengthening effect of observer talk within a close family:

> I'm from a very confident, almost cocky business background.
> ... When we left home in the morning, nobody was left at home, everybody went into the world, into the marketplace. At the end of the day, you came back, shut the fortress door and all discussed how you'd got on. You licked your wounds and got ready to go out again next day. There was a great feeling of 'US' against the world.
>
> Burr, 1986: 22

When relationships are flourishing, observer talk can nourish and sustain. Where there is bitterness or unresolved conflict, however, it can easily break down. For a parent resentful at bearing sole responsibility for the day-to-day care of the children, for instance, recounting the events of the day may include a strong 'participant' dimension as she uses the minor disasters narrowly averted to say, directly or indirectly: 'Why weren't you here? 'Why do you leave it all to me?' 'Why don't you give me the support I need?'

The result may be an argument as the partner protests: 'I've had a lot of work'. 'You don't know what it's like'. 'Don't you ever think of anyone but yourself?' 'Observer' language may swiftly become 'participant' language as each tries to get at the other with words.

The ebb and flow between 'participant' and 'observer' language is often most strikingly evident when relationships are floundering. At such times people sometimes turn to counselling for help. Counselling, along with psychotherapy – the talking cure in all its myriad forms – is only possible at all because we are able to talk *about* what we did as well as doing it, talk *about* feelings as well as feeling them, *about* relationships as well as living them.

In counselling sessions talk often moves rapidly to and fro between 'participant' and 'observer' poles. These extracts are from a conversation between a middle-class American couple, Mr and Mrs E who had gone to a therapist for help as their relationship began to go wrong. Much of their talk centres on the handling of their four children – three were adolescents and one four years old when this conversation took place in the presence of their therapist. For them, unlike the idealised case, the switch to 'observer' language was not easy to sustain:

Mr E: So, you agree then, that child management is a situation where we both should be . . . ah . . . consistent?

An attempt to stand back as an observer, take stock, establish what he and his wife agree on. His attempt, however, is thwarted almost immediately by Mrs E who hesitates no more than a moment before introducing a less detached note:

Mrs E: Well, I think it for a . . . yes, I do. And I also think that you have it blown up into something that is ridiculous.

An accusation to which her husband responds with a counter-accusation, 'participating' now, no longer trying to stand back:

Mr E: You think it's a lot bigger item with me than it is to you. And yet, you complain to me that the children have no respect for you whatsoever.

This opens the floodgates:

Mrs E: Well, if I can't complain to you who am I going to complain to?
Mr E: The children.
Mrs E: Oh, well, then you don't want to be complained to.
Mr E: No, I'm not saying that at all. I'm saying to you that if

> you feel that you don't have the respect of child *A*, that
> you should tell child *A* . . .
>
> Thomas, 1977: 179

The brief attempt by Mr *E* to stand back, establish common
ground, look at their differences together is not supported by his
wife and rapidly breaks down as participant language takes over
and the couple begin to quarrel. Though they are talking about
their past behaviour – the stuff of 'observer' talk – they are not
'observers'. Instead their view of one another's past behaviour
provides ammunition for the row in which both participate
whole-heartedly.

Mr *E* makes a further attempt to take on an observer role:

> Mr *E*:   The issue is that complaints [to him about the chil-
>   dren's behaviour] are raised . . . quite some time after
>   the fact . . .

This effort, however, fails even more dismally than the last as his
wife responds as a participant, reacting impatiently to his use of
the word 'complaint':

> Mrs *E*:   (Shrilly, exasperated, and loudly) It's not a complaint! I
>   just finished telling you that!

Mr *E* abandons his 'observer' role and participates in the ensuing
quarrel:

> Mr *E*:   How am I supposed to know?
> Mrs *E*:   Oh! (Exasperated)
> Mr *E*:   How am I supposed to know?
> Mrs *E*:   I don't know how you're supposed to know. I suppose
>   I have to tell you ahead of time this isn't a com-
>   plaint . . .

Here Mrs *E* introduces a note of sarcasm, a form of attack that is a
clear mark of participant language. From there she makes an
enormous leap back to her main grievance:

Mrs E: . . . In other words, you really don't want to discuss
         the children.
Mr E: That's not the fact at all.
Mrs E: Well, it must be! Because apparently, if it's discussing,
         it's complaining.

Thomas, 1977: 180–1

Attempts to interpret the transcript of Mr and Mrs E's conversation are hampered because we have only the words, not the tone,
nor the way they looked at one another, or turned away, or paced
around. This restriction aside, however, a way of looking at their
talk is to see Mr E as a man repeatedly attempting to stand back
from his domestic situation, trying to state the problems between
him and his wife, struggling to assume an 'observer' role. A way of
looking at Mrs E is to see her as constantly thwarting her
husband's efforts; to see her as locked by bitterness and resentment into a 'participant' role that causes her to persist with the
quarrels and disagreements that brought the couple to the therapist in the first place.

If we look more closely at the nature of Mr E's attempts to stand
back, however, then some of the limitations of the 'observer' role
become apparent. Certainly he appears to be trying to take stock
by putting problems into words: 'The issue is . . . ', 'Let me define
it properly . . . ', 'Let me put it to you this way . . . ' A closer
examination of what he says though shows him concentrating on
his wife's behaviour and reactions rather than his own: ' . . . of
late you've thrown it up at me that . . . ', 'you are not prepared to
come to grips with the situation of child . . . management'. A
good deal of Mrs E's hostile participant response then appears to
be provoked by what she sees as misrepresentations of her
position:

Mr E: . . . the fact that you're mad at me is the fact that you
         are also mad at yourself . . .
Mrs E: No, I'm not mad at myself.
Mr E: Mad at yourself because you don't have the children's
         respect.
Mrs E: I'm not mad. What are you talking about respect for?
         (Silence) What I was talking about had nothing to do
         with respect whatsoever.

Thomas, 1977: 183

Though the capacity to use language as an 'observer' – standing back, taking stock – is an indispensable and vital function, there can be no guarantee that it necessarily provides a basis for convergence. To converge upon what the other has in mind, to begin to understand, the observer needs to listen to, not just hear, the views of the observed.

'When people come in to talk about a problem they don't generally have difficulty talking about it from their own point of view', a social worker commented. 'The problem is to get them to see it from someone else's. It can be very difficult for them to grasp another perspective'. Mr *E* illustrates this as he repeatedly gives *his* view of his wife's behaviour and its shortcomings. Unable to stand back and see his own from hers.

Perhaps this should not be surprising. Trapped in our own heads, we can never know for certain what it feels like to be anyone else. One of the limitations of observer language is that, if not used wisely, it can reinforce our isolation. If we judge others purely from our own point of view. Take stock only of *our* feelings about *their* behaviour. Take no account of the effects of our behaviour on them.

There are people, too, who have only very limited experience of adopting an 'observer' role, of talking *about* feelings and reactions in addition to feeling and reacting. 'Some couples rarely use language to communicate with each other about anything but mundane, concrete subjects', one marriage guidance counsellor said. 'Sometimes they have no idea the other may have had a different point of view. It's never occurred to either of them to talk about it'.

We have all been guilty of assuming without question that others know how we feel, of failing to see the need to explain. When others have upset us or made us angry, it is only too tempting to take it for granted they know what it is about their behaviour that bothers us so much. It is remarkably difficult to keep in mind that they do not necessarily see their behaviour the way we see it. We may be upset at what they have done – quite justifiably in our view. We forget that what they did may look very different from their perspective. They may genuinely not be able to see how it could upset us. Unless we try to explain.

A young couple consulted a marriage guidance counsellor in an effort to save their relationship. During their counselling it emerged that three or four years earlier the wife had had a brief affair with another man. At the time they had not talked much about the affair and she had all but forgotten about it. Yet he, it turned out, still felt deeply hurt though he had never once mentioned his feelings. Suffering in silence he had nevertheless assumed she knew that he was suffering, why he was suffering. When he finally did explain what he still felt, both were amazed: she that he still cared, he that she had forgotten. Telling her did not immediately heal his hurt. But without 'observer' language, without the capacity to talk *about*, she could never have known. Even the possibility of healing would have been denied.

This use of language we have called 'observer use' is complex, many-sided. Between people divided by unresolved conflict or bitterness – couples such as Mr and Mrs E – it can be difficult to sustain. Without it though we would be infinitely the poorer, in spite of its limitations. 'Observer' language opens up the possibility of our understanding what would otherwise be hidden. A faint possibility in some cases. But a possibility none the less.

We cannot read each other's minds. We do not necessarily understand another's distress, unless they give us some clue. Tears, or sighs, hunched shoulders, flatness of tone, all these are clues, but only to the fact of their feelings. We need words to know the cause. We may not always fully understand the words. But they are still a powerful means of allowing us a glimpse of another's private world.

21

Telling Stories: a special case of observer language

At the heart of the 'observer' use of language is our need to make some sense of the world we experience. Standing back and talking *about* what has happened to us as 'participants', *about* what we have seen or heard, assessing what others said or did, justifying ourselves perhaps – these are ways we try through language to make our experience intelligible.

One of the commonest ways we do this is by telling stories. There are many kinds of stories we tell, most of them not particularly memorable or momentous. We tell stories every time we recount some incident that happened at work, or in the supermarket, or in that appalling traffic jam, or what the boss said at the meeting, or what happened last year on holiday, or last week at the Job Centre. What we saw in the street, what we heard reported in the news.

Though many of the stories we tell and hear are soon forgotten, there are some stories that can have an enormous impact on tellers and listeners alike. These are the stories some of us never tell, stories of painful, sometimes shameful, experiences, stories of hurting and being hurt, of suffering or making others suffer.

Sometimes such stories are told within one of the ever-increasing number of self-help or mutual support groups. Such groups draw a great deal of their strength from the willingness of members to tell their personal stories of illness or loss, of addiction or inadequacy, to use talk to make public what they have privately undergone.

One of the reasons members of such groups are willing to tell their stories, acknowledge their feelings, reveal their regret or grief or guilt is that they are talking to people who are likely to understand. For a newcomer, hearing another's story can precipitate that overwhelming sense of relief that comes from realising you are not, after all, alone, that the desolate, terrifying, painful, perhaps humiliating experience you have endured does not separate you from the whole of mankind.

This recognition can sometimes be a turning-point, sometimes a very late turning-point, in the lives of many who experience it. One support group that has relied heavily on such 'observer' language for over half a century is Alcoholics Anonymous. AA was set up in the 1930s in Akron, Ohio, after local physician and longtime alcoholic, Robert Holbrook Smith, had been helped to overcome his dependence on drink by a visiting New York stockbroker, William Wilson. Wilson was himself a former alcoholic who had been supported in his search for sobriety by his involvement in the Oxford Group, a religious movement for moral rearmament.

From Wilson's success with Smith was born the conviction that one alcoholic can help and influence another in a way no non-alcoholic can. This conviction underlies the personal accounts from former alcoholics that make up more than half of the basic AA book, *Alcoholics Anonymous*. One account reads: 'he was the first living human with whom I had ever talked, who knew what he was talking about in regard to alcoholism from actual experience. In other words, he talked my language' (AA, 1957: 192).

Today AA is a worldwide organisation, its success in helping large numbers of people conquer alcohol dependence acknowledged even by its critics. AA's religious, or at any rate, 'spiritual' approach does not suit everyone, but for those who do respond, talk is one of the chief mechanisms for change.

When, a few years ago, David Robinson made a detailed study of AA, he called the book that comes out of it: *Talking out of Alcoholism: the self-help process of Alcoholics Anonymous*. Not, he acknowledged, that talk came easily to everyone:

Some people find it difficult but everybody knows how important it is, because it is only through talk, and AA's special kind of talking, that 'newcomers' can share and understand what AA is and 'old timers' can carry the AA message to those they think should hear it.

Robinson, 1979: 118

In the course of his research Robinson talked to the UK General Secretary of AA who confirmed his view of the enormous significance of talk:

All we can hope to do, by talking about a person's experience is change his attitude . . . Who am I to say he is wrong? I must be tolerant and accept that this is how he is thinking. It may be a barrier to his recovery and all I can hope to do is influence his thinking and outlook . . . by talking. You kick a ball around long enough and you'll have a game, won't you? Talk, talk, talk and because you talk you start a man thinking.

Robinson, 1979: 63

The most characteristic type of AA talk is undoubtedly the telling of personal stories. When an established member of AA approaches a potential member (known as Twelfth Stepping) he may tell the story of his own drinking experience – how he started, what he was like when drunk, how his drinking affected his family and work: 'The aim,' Robinson says, 'is to get the potential member to listen to the experiences of the AA member and to see so much of himself in the story that he "realises" that if the AA member is "an alcoholic" then "I must be an alcoholic too"'.

One AA member described this process:

he told me his drinking story. And I began to pick it up and think, 'Oh yes'. You can identify with different things that he may have done or felt. 'Oh, I've done them as well' you think . . . . It was as if he'd opened up my little brain and was reading my lot.

Robinson, 1979: 45–6

If the new recruit goes on to attend meetings of AA he or she will hear many such stories and will probably tell their own. In the AA way of talk the personal story is the most important means whereby members come to see that their individual experience of drinking and its effects upon their lives and the lives of those close to them, however terrible and humiliating, is not unique. Hearing a personal story can break the conviction of absolute isolation.

The special character of AA personal stories is that they are not told primarily in order to establish a simple convergence between

speaker and hearer meanings. Told successfully their chief effect is
not so much that the listener comes to understand the teller as that
the listener comes to understand his own experience better.
Robinson reports Bean, an earlier AA researcher, as suggesting
that this is a process of 'empathising in reverse': 'to empathise in
reverse, to feel that what the speaker experienced can be meaningful to yourself and feel what he felt, not so that you can better
understand him, but so that you can accept yourself' (Robinson,
1979: 68).

The lines of communication in this kind of 'observer' talk are
not drawn, as they usually are, from speaker and speaker's
meaning to hearer and hearer's understanding of speaker's meaning. Instead they run from speaker and speaker's meaning to
hearer and hearer's understanding of hearer's experience. Convergence, if it occurs, is oblique.

'Empathising in reverse' works because so many of the stories
are in essence very similar. Not all newcomers understand that an
essential part of AA talk is saying things which are 'the same as
everybody else'. Some feel the need to dramatise, afraid their
stories are too commonplace, too much like others to warrant
telling without embroidery.

It can take time to see that telling your personal story within AA
means offering the group your own version of what everyone has
experienced. Doing so may be a step in your own recovery and in
the recovery of your listeners. To be able to tell your story you
have been forced to look at your past, acknowledge it and begin to
distance yourself from it, while at the same time providing
listeners with one more experience with which to identify. For the
overall process to work, however, listeners must also be prepared
to play their part as tellers, not because their stories are different to
the others, but because they are essentially the same.

Of course all stories do not affect all listeners equally or in the
same way. Listeners will themselves be in different states, some
much further than others along the road to recovery. Robinson's
survey showed, however, that around half the members polled
gained something from all stories, while almost all listened to
stories until they found something useful. And when he asked
members what they got most out of AA meetings: 'hearing talk
and stories' and 'discussion groups' were at the top of the list.

'Observer' talk, however, does not always work. Part of the
value of David Robinson's research was to reveal a fuller picture of

the effects of telling and hearing stories. Some, like John, for instance, felt the emphasis on personal stories was, in the end, depressing:

> It depresses me. The whole idea's a good thing, I think, but the meetings themselves depress me. It's all the bloody same. It was a repeat. In the group I was in you began to memorise every-body's history and it just depressed me.
>
> Robinson, 1979: 69

Robinson's survey of AA members revealed, behind the general enthusiasm for story-telling, other criticisms of the way they were sometimes told: dwelling in over-much detail on past drinking history, for instance, was thought unhelpful, as was members 'theorising' about why they had become alcoholics, or telling stories in a rambling, inconsequential way, or forgetting everyone else in the room.

These comments suggest that members had a sense of an appropriate way of telling one's personal story. A researcher working with Robinson, Stuart Henry, observed after sitting in on an AA meeting:

> I noticed a characteristic style of presentation of 'the story'. It involves continually closing one's eyes and then opening them, sometimes pausing with eyes closed, sometimes talking with eyes closed, always talking slowly in a controlled way and seriously. Also apparent is the manner of delivery, i.e. repeating lines so as to add emphasis. It would appear that there may be a learned 'art' of giving a biographical account.
>
> Robinson, 1979: 48

This 'learned art' may not be so much a specific technique as learning to tell one's story in a way listeners can share.

Over time, and with longer active involvement in AA, members often begin to view their past differently and their stories begin to change. This should not be surprising. Stories are not 'the truth once and for all' but rather a way of looking at the past. If there is a shift in perspective, then stories are bound to shift too. Robinson found, for instance, a change in the emphasis of personal stories from problems of drinking to problems of recovery. In time the drinking experience may be only briefly mentioned or even not at all as members dwell more on their experience of AA itself.

With the change in emphasis may go a change in group. One member explained:

> I went over to another group on Saturday. I did mainly recovery. I said 'I'm not gonna do my drinking story. I've done it and I've done it'. One or two nodded in a knowledgeable way knowing that they'd done the same thing and they were thinking 'Thank God'. It can get much too easy. So we didn't do that and I spoke on recovery.
>
> Robinson, 1979: 102

For more established members of AA, observer talk begins to be less a means of coming to terms with the drinking experience and more a question of assessing and evaluating the overall experience they have had within AA. Through talk their past experience is received and evaluated in relation to a present that has come to include the experience of AA.

Although in the AA way of talk observer language predominates – recounting and reviewing, embroidering, commenting and evaluating – it is nevertheless striking that the prelude to all this observer talk is a crucial piece of participant language. The newcomer to an AA meeting makes a public declaration as a participant: 'I am an alcoholic'.

Some members report that the sense of relief on publicly admitting their private problem is their single most important experience in AA. Discovering that they are neither 'alone' nor 'unique' has been described as heartening, gladdening, reassuring, comforting. In time, not only relief accompanies the declaration. As Griffith Edwards said: 'To be able to say "and I'm an alcoholic" without embarrassment, and perhaps sometimes it seems with a certain inflection of pride, is the badge of the AA member' (Edwards, 1964).

With this 'participant' step the AA member embarks on a long journey conducted largely through 'observer' talk.

22

Telling Stories and Telling the Truth

'Men live upon trust.'
John Locke

Telling and hearing stories as part of coming to terms with difficult and painful experiences is one of the most striking instances of the power and value of observer language. It is, though, only one of the many and varied reasons we recount to one another 'what happened' in story form.

Sometimes we tell our tales with an eye to the audience, exaggerating, embroidering, dramatising to provoke a reaction. Some are first-hand stories: 'I saw it with my own eyes. She was paddling around the golfish pond in the park, waving a Union Jack, stone-cold sober . . . ' Others are second or third-hand, stories we have heard from others, often about people we do not know at all. 'There was this woman, apparently, who was allergic to dandelions . . . '

Again when life has lightly stepped on us or put us firmly down, telling 'what happened' as a story can pick us up, help redress the balance, patch up our self-image. A patient, for instance, may emerge from a visit to the doctor dissatisfied, baffled, frustrated, feeling they have been side-tracked, unable to get their point across. Like the woman reported in Webb and Stimson's research on consultations between patients and doctors – the following is an extract from her 'story' of a consultation with her GP:

he said 'I'm giving you some ointment and some tablets'. I said 'What are the tablets for doctor?' And he said 'To ease the pain'. 'Oh well, I don't want tablets for the pain, it's not that bad'. 'Oh alright' he said . . . So then the interview was over as far as he was concerned. But I wasn't at all satisfied. I said 'Well what

164

about the dizzy spells I've been having, doctor?' And he just sat back and looked at me in silence, staring into my face – thinking of something to say I suppose. So to help him I said 'Do you think it could be my age?' because whatever you've got wrong with you past the age of thirty-five it's always your 'age', and he paused and said 'Well let's put it this way, none of us is getting a day younger are we?' Very profound, I thought . . . Well, I left the doctor's feeling I just needn't have bothered going. I was thoroughly dissatisfied and I'm none the wiser.

Webb and Stimson, 1976: 119

A prominent feature of this story is the way the patient apparently dominated the consultation, rejecting the doctor's prescription: 'I don't want tablets for the pain . . . '; prolonging the interview – 'What about the dizzy spells I've been having?'; guiding the diagnosis: 'Do you think it could be my age?'. The doctor is depicted as dull-witted: ' . . . looked at me in silence . . . . thinking of something to say, I suppose', if not downright stupid: 'Very profound, I thought'.

Webb and Stimson observed many consultations, concluding that, whatever they may say in their stories, patients are generally much less active and directive than doctors. The emphasis on the active part played by patients in their stories after the event they suggest 'owes more to the story being a vehicle for making the patient appear rational and sensible, and for redressing the imbalance between patient and doctor, than it does to the event itself' (Webb and Stimson, 1976: 111).

Stories, in other words, allow us to tell it, not necessarily as we recall it, but rather the way we would have liked it to be, the way it was in our heads, privately, the way we reconstructed it to ourselves afterwards. Certainly not, in this case, the way the doctor would have told it.

In telling her story after the event this patient was free from the checks and constraints 'participant' language involves. Where at the time we might have been tense, ill-at-ease, the doctor preoc-cupied or bored, in the telling she figures prominently, confident, even magisterial.

When we tell stories we are in control, free to select which elements to include, which to leave out, according to the effect we want to create. A mature student went for an interview for a research fellowship some years ago to an Oxbridge women's college. Chatting with a couple of friends afterwards she told her story of 'what happened', first the interview itself, then the dinner that followed:

Teller:	and then coffee in the Senior Common Room afterwards and conversation went like this – this sort of conversation – have you noticed, President, that – um – the boiled eggs at Sunday breakfast are always
Friend A:	(Laughs)
Teller:	hard and President said 'Ah well, the simple truth is that if you're going to boil eggs communally they must be hard'. (Laughs)
Friends:	(Laugh)
Teller:	Everybody waited and she said, 'You see, you have to crack the head of an egg when you take it out of the pan otherwise it goes on cooking'. (Laughs)
Friend A:	(Laughs)
Teller:	And so we did eggs. Everybody made their contribution from all over the Senior Common Room about their point of view about eggs. There were some would rather have them much too soft than much too hard and some people would rather not have an egg at all and some people thought the thing to do was just put them in water and take them out again and then let them go on cooking without cracking their heads you know you got every possible point of view about boiled eggs then you went on to the next
Friend A:	(Laughs)
Teller:	topic it was like as though there was an unwritten agenda.

Svartvik and Quirk, 1980: 96–7

Story-telling by a participant-turned-observer, unconstrained by other participants' views of what took place. A tale not strictly 'how it was' but rather told for laughs to an audience looking to be amused. Story-telling used to consolidate relationships, the teller encouraged by the laughter to exploit her tale, build up the discussion on eggs. Make a good story out of it.

Assessing 'what *really* happened' is made more difficult by the ease with which fantasy enters into our stories. Telling stories to family and friends of how we want them to believe it was, telling stories in public, out loud, is only an extension of the stories we tell ourselves in private. Inside, each of us has flattened controversial opponents with masterly arguments, untangled the critical problems of the day with an incisive proposal that brooked no objection, been projected into national prominence with a speech that turned the tide, been attacked, humiliated, exposed, played a heroic part in some tale of danger and last-minute rescue, and so on and so on.

In these fantastic stories we tell ourselves, mostly in private, we give expression to preoccupations, fears, anxieties and, of course, desires that are perfectly real. Thurber captured some of the simpler male preoccupations in *The Secret Life of Walter Mitty*, with its fantasies of unflamboyant courage, heroic modesty, sexual conquest, high living and high gambling.

Stories allow us to depict our cast as we will, and as a consequence we can in the telling begin to get our own back, justly or unjustly, on those who have slighted or annoyed or angered us: 'I was annoyed with our own doctor', Webb and Stimson report a woman saying about her father's illness:

> we kept the truth from my mother and the callous bugger stood in the passage one day when she called him in and he said, 'Of course you know you haven't got him much longer, you know what he's got don't you', 'No,' she said, 'I've got no idea'. 'Well, he's got cancer, and there's nothing you can do for him'.
>
> Stimson and Webb, 1975: 100

A story, this one, which is already second-hand, the woman reporting her mother's account of what the doctor had said as he stood in the passage. We cannot know how far it is fantasy and how far 'what really happened'. Was the doctor actually insensitive or did he in fact tell the storyteller's mother as gently as he could that her husband had cancer, in the sincere belief it was time she knew? Was the mother's original account of 'what happened', of what the doctor said, how he said it, itself coloured by shock or disbelief? Was the doctor's real offence to go against the wishes of the family: 'we kept the truth from my mother . . .', those he offended using story-telling as a weapon of revenge.

Take the following comparison between the 'marvellous' Dr Fletcher and the 'dreadful' Dr Bailey:

Dr Fletcher is marvellous. I've got complete confidence in him, I trust him completely. Anything he says, that's right by me. Now Bailey I don't like. There was a time when I had this terrible pain in my back. I was dragging myself around – I had to go on because of the baby, but it went on and on, it was driving me mad, I couldn't stand it any more. So my husband called for the doctor, and Fletcher couldn't come, it was Bailey's day for home visits. And honestly, without a word of a lie, he was in the door, took one look at me, and said 'Lumbago, you'll have to take it easy'. That's all he said and was gone. I didn't have a chance to ask anything, nor did my husband, he was out of the house too fast. We just looked at each other in amazement.

Stimson and Webb, 1975: 104

Did Dr Bailey's behaviour reinforce the image, already well-established within this household, of one doctor, Fletcher, who was inevitably 'marvellous', the other, Bailey, unfailingly 'dreadful'? Was the story told to further reinforce the image? Was Dr Bailey doomed from the moment he arrived to be depicted as 'dreadful'? Did the practice have other patients for whom the judgements may have been reversed: 'dreadful' Fletcher, 'marvellous' Bailey?

Why should we be constantly telling stories about what we undergo? Why do we not just tell it as it is? These were the questions Bishop Butler raised in *The Sermon on the Character of Balaam*: 'Things and actions are what they are and the consequences of them will be what they will be; why, then, should we desire to be deceived?'

The answer is not difficult to find when so many 'things and actions' are disquieting, distressing, often painful. Stories are one of the ways we deceive ourselves and are deceived. They provide a means of reconstructing our experiences as we will, creating fantasies that may be far removed from 'what really happened', bathing the world in a warmer glow, a softer radiance than it customarily presents.

Nevertheless there must remain dangers in telling stories that drive a wedge between the worlds we construct and the world we have to participate in. 'Honestly, without a word of a lie', the storyteller assured her listeners. When we tell stories we are not usually lying. Exaggerating, perhaps, but not lying. How far, though, can we be said to be telling the truth?

In asking such a question we draw close to a central paradox of observer language: the stories we tell, the accounts we give of 'what happened', can serve as much to deceive – ourselves and others – as to enlighten. We all individually construct images of the world and our place in it, our stories often not so much 'what really happened' as versions of what we recall tailored, wittingly or unwittingly, to fit the images we have already made.

In trying to understand human affairs, unlike trying to understand the natural world, arriving at what we agree is the case is unavoidably mixed with tacit and largely unacknowledged beliefs and values. The considerable power and sometimes spectacular success of the natural sciences in our times depends upon those practising them having come to pretty good agreement about the kinds of detailed tests and procedures to determine in a given case what actually took place and what can be predicted as a consequence.

Pretty good agreement, but, of course, not perfect. There will still be some, though fewer, tacit and unacknowledged beliefs and values lurking in the background as the existence of different interpretations and passionate controversies in most branches of the natural sciences reminds us.

Outside the natural sciences, though, both within the human sciences and in everyday life, we have few well-established tests and procedures. Instead we must rely on trust. Because language allows us to tell what version we will of 'what happened', we have to trust each other to curb our fantasies, to keep our stories as close as we can, on those occasions when it matters, to the way we recall it was.

This would not be so difficult if we were the rational and co-operative creatures we are so often imagined to be, particularly by some philosophers and linguists writing on truth and meaning. It is not, of course, that we cannot at times be rational and co-operative. Rather a great deal of communication takes place in contexts where self-image and the desire to impress, to persuade, to convince, to placate, to alarm, to annoy, are far more influential than reason in deciding what we say and what we understand by what others say.

Swift, in the fourth book of *Gulliver's Travels*, imagined what communication would be like if we actually were rational and co-operative, only interested in talking about things and actions as, in Butler's phrase 'they are'. In *A Voyage to the Country of the*

Houyhnhnms, he created two races, the Houyhnhnms, rational and virtuous, and the Yahoos, passionate and vicious. Gulliver was one of us, a Yahoo, but taken up by the Houyhnhnms because he was 'endowed with some Rudiments of Reason', 'a small Pittance' of intelligence.

Through Gulliver, Swift extols: 'The wise and virtuous Houyhnhnms, who abound in all the excellencies that can adorn a Rational Creature . . .' and: '. . . who live under the Government of Reason . . .'

Furthermore the etymology of the unpronounceable Houyhnhnms – 'The Word *Houyhnhnm* in their Tongue signifies a Horse; and in its Etymology, *the Perfection of Nature*' – leaves us in no doubt that Swift intended them to represent a higher form of life than the revolting Yahoos – a thinly-disguised portrait of all that Swift found most disgusting and despicable in the human race: 'Upon the whole I never beheld in all my Travels so disagreeable an Animal, or one against which I naturally conceived so strong an Antipathy' (Part IV, Ch. 1).

Beneath the cool prose Swift's fiery and abrasive satire is chiefly directed at the pride, the folly and the vanity of humankind. But language, particularly where this involves telling the truth or lying does not escape his lash.

In Chapter IV, on the Houyhnhnms' 'Notions of Truth and Falsehood', Gulliver discovers that the language of his Master, for so he chose to call the Dapple-Grey Horse that had befriended him, had a curious lacuna: ' . . . having Occasion to talk of *Lying and False Representation*, it was with much difficulty that he comprehended what I meant; although he had otherwise a most acute Judgement'.

These difficulties arose because for a Houyhnhnm:

> the Use of Speech was to make us understand one another, and to receive Information of Facts; now if any one said *the Thing which was not*, these Ends were defeated; because I cannot properly be said to understand him; and I am so far from receiving information, that he leaves me worse than in Ignorance . . . I am led to believe a Thing *Black* when it is *White*, and *Short* when it is *Long*.

These, Gulliver concludes: ' . . . were all the Notions he had concerning that Faculty of *Lying*, so perfectly well understood, and so universally practised among human Creatures' (Part IV, Ch. 4).

Idealising the rational, never-lying Houyhnhnms as he does, however, Gulliver fails to notice that inseparable from the absence of the capacity to tell a lie goes a corresponding absence of the capacity to tell the truth. Without choice the Houyhnhnms, in effect, tell neither.

Denis de Rougemont once remarked that man alone among the animals can lie. He might as strikingly have said that man alone among the animals can tell the truth, since man alone has a language with an observer dimension allowing him to recall, relive and recast his experience as he chooses. It might be more accurate to say that man alone among the animals can purposely deceive others because he has the capacity to lie, the capacity to say *the Thing which is not*. Much as Swift, and we at times, might wish it otherwise, we cannot have one without the other.

The great strength of 'observer' language and its greatest limitation lies in its providing equally for us to tell it 'as it was' and to tell it 'as we want it to appear'. Language does not come neatly labelled 'true' or 'false', 'reliable' or 'unreliable'. The same language allows us to give a reasonable approximation or a complete distortion of 'what really happened'.

Under such conditions, for observer language to work at all, for us to be able to rely on what we are told, we need, in addition to Locke's two secret references, a third, a final secret reference: a tacit assumption of sincerity. We need to be confident that, on those occasions where it matters, the stories we are told, the accounts we are given, the reports we hear are as true and faithful as the teller can make them. Which are 'the occasions where it matters' it is up to each of us to judge.

The importance of the largely unacknowledged final secret reference is its ensuring that, where it matters, we can have trust in what we hear. Without such trust, communication would not work.

'Men,' Locke rightly said, 'live upon trust'. And nowhere more implicitly than in their use of language. Language: ' . . . the great Instrument, and common Tye of Society' (III, I, 1) depends upon implicit trust in each other's sincere efforts to tell it as it was.

Acts of lying, false representation, telling it as it was not, loosen the bonds that language ties amongst us, undermining bit by bit the trust on which we depend. The skilled liar flourishes best where trust in truthfulness is most firmly established.

Paradoxically, where it does not matter, 'white' lies, stories told with an eye to the audience, hype of all kinds, telling as it is not, can extend and enrich our lives in a way the rational and humourless Houyhnhnms could not have begun to understand.

But in the end, each saying of *the Thing which is not*, at times when sincerity is called for, begins to destroy the implicit trust communication is built upon. The effective working of language as a bridge between us ultimately relies upon a double bind: a personal commitment to telling it as we believe it was; a personal faith that others are doing the same.

Where it matters we must, for language to work, be able to trust in each other's sincerity: the ultimate secret reference. Where we fail that trust:

> Things fall apart; the centre cannot hold;
> Mere anarchy is loosed upon the world,
>
> W. B. Yeats, *The Second Coming*

Coda

Adapted, in homage, from Locke:

When we have Surveyed the Limits of what we can do with Language, and made some Estimate of our ability to Understand and make ourselves Understood, we shall not be inclined to sit still and not set our Thoughts on work at all, in Despair of Understanding anything because we cannot Understand everything.

'Tis of great use to a Sailor to know the length of his line, though he cannot with it fathom all the depth of the Ocean. 'Tis well he knows, that it is long enough to reach the bottom, at such places as are necessary to direct his Voyage. Our Business therefore is not to understand all things but those which concern our Conduct. If we can find out those Measures whereby a thoughtful Creature, put in that State which Man is, in this World, may and ought to govern his Opinions, and Actions depending thereon, we need not be troubled that some other things escape our Understanding.

References

AARSLEFF, H., *From Locke to Saussure* (Athlone, 1982).

Alcoholics Anonymous (The World's Work Ltd, 1957).

Annual Report of the Lay Observer (1984 and 1985).

ATKINSON, P., 'The Problem of Grey Hair', in *Uttering, Muttering*, ed. C. Adelman (Bulmershe College of Higher Education, 1978).

ATKINSON, P., *The Clinical Experience. The Construction and Reconstruction of Medical Reality* (Gower, 1981).

BANKS SMITH, N., 'The Pain beyond Words', *The Guardian*, 13 May 1985.

BATESON, P. P. G., 'Testing an Observer's Ability to Identify Individual Animals', *Animal Behaviour*, 25 (1977): 247–8.

BENTLEY, V., 'Ungaro. A Passion for Perfume', *Woman's Journal*, August 1986.

BERLINS, M., 'Digging for Real Gold in the Hills', *The Times*, 7 May 1984.

BIDMEAD, C., 'A Night to Put the Knife into the Mac Pack's Dreams', *The Guardian*, 10 April 1986.

BORGES, J. L., 'Of Exactitude in Science', in *A Universal History of Infamy*, trans. Norman Thomas di Giovanni (Penguin Books, 1975).

BOSTON, R., 'How Old Pals Reached Incandescence on the Meejah', *The Guardian*, 14 March 1986.

BRITTON, J., *Language and Learning* (Allen Lane, The Penguin Press, 1970).

BROADBENT, M., *Michael Broadbent's Pocket Guide to Wine-Tasting* (Mitchell Beazley, 1982).

BURR, R., *Female Tycoons* (Rosters Ltd, 1986).

BUTLER, J., *Fifteen Sermons*, ed. T. A. Roberts (SPCK, 1970).

BYRD, R. E., *Alone* (Putnam, 1938).

CARROLL, L., *The Complete Works of Lewis Carroll* (Nonesuch Press, 1939).

COMMITTEE OF VICE-CHANCELLORS AND PRINCIPALS, *Academic Standards in Universities* (July 1986).

COULTHARD, M. and ASHBY, M., 'A Linguistic Description of Doctor-Patient Interviews', in M. Wadsworth and D. Robinson, *Studies in Everyday Medical Life* (Martin Robertson, 1976).

DAVIES, G., 'Face Recall Systems', in *Perceiving and Remembering Faces*, ed. G. Davies, H. Ellis and J. Shepherd (Academic Press, 1981).

DAYANANDA, J. T., 'Plain English in the United States', *English Today*, January 1986, 13–16.

DUNN, D., 'The Beautiful Fairy Godmother', *Sunday Times Magazine*, 26 January 1986.

EDWARDS, G., 'The Puzzle of AA', *New Society*, 28 May 1964.

ELLIS, H., 'Theoretical Aspects of Face Recognition', in *Perceiving and Remembering Faces*, ed. G. Davies, H. Ellis and J. Shepherd (Academic Press, 1981).

FINDLAY, J., 'Goedelian Sentences: A Non-Numerical Approach', *Mind*, (1942): 259–65.

FISHER, M. F. K., *Brillat-Savarin's The Physiology of Taste* (Alfred A. Knopf, 1971).

FLINT, J., 'Clear Signal – to the Wise', *The Times*, 17 February 1986.

GANNAWAY, H., 'Making Sense of School', in *Explorations in Classroom Observation*, ed. M. Stubbs and S. Delamont (John Wiley, 1976).

GOLDING, W., *The Inheritors* (Faber and Faber, 1961).

GOLDSTEIN, A. and CHANCE, J., 'Laboratory Studies of Face Recognition', in *Perceiving and Remembering Faces*, ed. G. Davies, H. Ellis and J. Shepherd (Academic Press, 1981).

GOMBRICH, E. H., 'The Mask and the Face: The Perception of Physiognomic Likeness in Life and in Art', in *Art, Perception and Reality*, ed. E. H. Gombrich, J. Hochberg and M. Black (Johns Hopkins University Press, 1972).

HART-DAVIS, D., 'Country Matters', *The Independent*, 11 October 1986.

HAVILAND, J. B., *Gossip, Reputation and Knowledge in Zinacantan* (University of Chicago Press, 1977).

HERTZ, L., *The Business Amazons* (Andre Deutsch, 1986).

JOHNSON, F. and ARIES, E., 'The Talk of Women Friends', *Women's Studies International Forum* (1983): 353–61.

JONES, B., 'Considered Opinions', *Sunday Times Magazine*, 11 December 1977.

KEE, C., 'The Book Stops Here', *The Guardian*, 22 June 1984.

LAWSON, H., 'TV-am: The Inside Story', *Observer*, 29 January 1984.

LEHRER, A., *Wine and Conversation* (Indiana University Press, 1983).

LOCKE, J., *An Essay concerning Human Understanding*, ed. Peter H. Nidditch (Clarendon Press, 1975). (Originally published 1689.)

LYNN, J. and JAY, A., *Yes Minister. The Diaries of a Cabinet Minister by the Rt Hon. James Hacker MP*, vol. 3, BBC, 1983.

MAHER, C. and CUTTS, M., 'Plain English in the United Kingdom', *English Today*, January 1986: 10–12.

MILL, J. S., *A System of Logic*, ed. J. M. Robson (Routledge & Kegan Paul, 1974).

ORWELL, G., 'Politics and the English Language', *Horizon*, April 1946.

PARKER, T., 'The Scars Left by the Flames', *Sunday Times Magazine*, 4 May 1986.

PEARSALL SMITH, L., 'More Trivia', in *All Trivia* (Constable, 1933).

PENRY, J., *Looking at Faces and Remembering Them. A Guide to Facial Identification* (Elek Books, 1971).

PIFF, C., *Let's Face It* (Sphere Books, 1986).

POLANYI, M., *Personal Knowledge, Towards a Post-Critical Philosophy* (Harper Torchbooks, 1964).

REES, S. and WALLACE, A., *Verdicts on Social Work* (Edward Arnold, 1982).

Report of the Commissioner of Police of the Metropolis for the year 1983 (HMSO, Cmnd 9268).

ROBINSON, D., *Talking out of Alcoholism. The Self-Help Process of Alcoholics Anonymous* (Croom Helm, 1979).

ROBINSON, J., *Masterglass. A Practical Course in Tasting Wine* (Pan Books, 1983).

ROBINSON, J., 'Know Your Grapes', *Sunday Times Magazine*, 7 September 1986.

SHEPHERD, J., DAVIES, G. and ELLIS, H., 'Studies in Cue Saliency', in *Perceiving and Remembering Faces*, ed. G. Davies, H. Ellis and J. Shepherd (Academic Press, 1981).

STIMSON, G. and WEBB, B., *Going to See the Doctor: the Consultation Process in General Practice* (Routledge & Kegan Paul, 1975).

STUBBS, M., *Language, Schools and Classrooms* (Methuen, 1976).

SVARTVIK, J. and QUIRK, R., *A Corpus of English Conversation*, Lund Studies in English, 56 (LiberLaromedel, 1980).

SWIFT, J., *Gulliver's Travels*, ed. John Hayward (Nonesuch Press, 1946).

TANNEN, D. and OZTEK, P. C., 'Health to our Mouths', in *Conversational Routine. Explorations in Standardized Communication Situations and Prepatterned Speech*, ed. F. Coulmas (Mouton, 1981).

TAYLOR, J., 'To Make it Easier for the Others', *The Guardian*, 22 May 1984.

THOMAS, E. J., *Marital Communication and Decision Making* (The Free Press, 1977).

TOYNBEE, P., 'Jungle Warfare', *The Guardian*, 29 December 1986.

VANDYKE PRICE, P., *The Taste of Wine* (Macdonald, 1976).

WALKER, R. and ADELMAN, C., 'Strawberries', in *Explorations in Classroom Observation*, ed. M. Stubbs and S. Delamont (John Wiley, 1976).

WEBB, B. and STIMSON, G., 'People's Accounts of Medical Encounters', in *Studies in Everyday Medical Life*, ed. M. Wadsworth and D. Robinson (Martin Robertson, 1976).

WHITEHEAD, A. N., *The Organisation of Thought: Educational and Scientific* (Williams & Norgate, 1917).

WITTGENSTEIN, L., *Philosophical Investigations*, trans. G. E. M. Anscombe (Macmillan 1953).

YOUNG, H., 'The Love that Dare Speak its Name too Often', *The Guardian*, 11 March 1986.

ZIJDERVELD, A. C., *On clichés. The Supersedure of Meaning by Function in Modernity* (Routledge & Kegan Paul, 1979).

Index

Aarsleff, H.   91
Adelman, C.   79, 80
Alcoholics Anonymous   80–1,
    159–63
animal communication   148–9
Ariès, E.   81
Arnold, M.   12
Ashby, M.   74
Atkinson, P.   105–9
Ausonius   10

Banks Smith, N.   136
Bateson, P. P. G.   87
Bentley, V.   129
Berlins, M.   81
Bertillon, A.   96
Bidmead, C.   57
Borges, J. L.   16, 17
Boston, R.   66
Brillat-Savarin   114
Britton, J.   25
Broadbent, M.   102, 112, 113,
    115, 116, 118
Buber, M.   25, 30, 33
Bühler, K.   146, 147
Burr, R.   152
Byrd, R.   77, 78, 79

Carroll, L.   17, 18, 29, 30, 35
Chance, J.   88
clichés   73
colour terms   105, 113
Condillac, E. B. de   91
Coulthard, M.   74
Cutts, M.   51

Darwin, C.   148
Davies, G.   90, 96–7
Dayananda, J. T.   54
Dunn, D.   34

Edwards, G.   163
Eliot, T. S.   12, 73

Ellis, H.   86, 90, 99
Epicurus   10

face-recall systems   96–100
Findlay, J.   82
Fisher, M. F. K.   114
Flint, J.   81–2

Gannaway, H.   62
Golding, W.   132, 149–51
Goldstein, A.   88
Gombrich, E. H.   88–9, 90
Goodall, J.   148–9
gossip   78

Hart-Davis, D.   128
Haviland, J. B.   77, 78
Herbert, G.   10
Hertz, L.   64–5
Hopkins, G. M.   11

Identikit   96, 97
insider talk   79–82

Jakobson, R.   146
jargon   101, 102
Jay, A.   53
Johnson, F.   81
Jones, B.   89

Kafka, F.   29
Kee, C.   127, 131

language and
    counselling   134, 136, 140–1,
        152–7
    emotion   133–41
    face recognition   86–92
    legal advice   137–40
    medical training   102–9
    perfume   129–30
    senses   85–132
    wine   111–25

179

language functions 146
language routines 70, 71–6
Lawson, H. 79
*Lay Observer, Report of
    the* 139–40
Lehrer, A. 121–7
Locke, J. 2, 32–6, 37, 39–44, 46–9,
    52, 56, 57, 59, 68, 119–20, 164,
    171, 173
Lynn, J. 53

Maher, C. 51
Marlowe, C. 12
meaning
  asymmetry 60, 74–5
  convergence/divergence 43,
    45–64, 70, 74, 77, 78, 82, 85,
    88, 89, 91, 93, 94, 102, 109,
    121, 125, 131, 134, 137, 138,
    139, 141, 156, 160, 161
  mind dependence 46
  privateness 32–4, 37, 47,
    117–20, 122, 146
  speaker/hearer meanings 44,
    46, 60–4, 71, 85, 88–91, 93,
    94, 126, 138, 161
  vagueness 40, 45, 53, 54, 56
  variability 40, 43, 45, 47
Mill, J. S. 41–2

naming 38–44

observer language 145–72
Orwell, G. 53, 54, 57
Oztek, P. C. 72

Parker, T. 136
part/whole relation 91–2, 129
participant language 145–72
Pearsall Smith, L. 56–7
Penry, J. 93, 97
Photofit 96, 97–100
Piff, C. 131
Polanyi, M. 012–3, 105, 111
portrait parlé 96–7
▪blic/private paradox 25–30

    R. 63, 166

Rees, S. 67–9, 136–7
Robinson, D. 80–1, 159–63
Robinson, J. 115, 116, 117, 118
Rougemont, D. de 171
Rubenstein, J. 137, 138

Sappho 9
Scott, D. 87, 102
secret reference 35, 37, 44, 45, 59,
    171, 172
self-help groups 158
Shakespeare, W. 128
Shepherd, J. 90, 99
Solicitors' Family Law
    Association 137, 138
solipsism 29, 30, 34, 35, 120
Stevens, W. 11
Stimson, G. 74, 75, 164–5, 167,
    168
Stoppard, T. 9
Stubbs, M. 75
Svartvik, J. 63, 166
Swift, J. 38, 39, 169–71

Tannen, D. 72
Taylor, J. 135
Thomas, E. J. 153–5
Thurber, J. 111,112, 167
Toynbee, P. 148–9
trigger words 112, 117, 118, 120,
    126

Vandyke Price, P. 117, 118, 119

Walker, R. 79, 80
Wallace, A. 67–9, 136–7
Webb, B. 74, 75, 164–5, 167, 168
Whitehead, A. N. 26, 55, 68
Wilson, W. 159
Wittgenstein, L. 3, 4, 7, 85, 92,
    133, 149

Yeats, W. B. 172
Young, H. 57

Zijderveld, A. 73